Richard Dayringer, ThD

Life Cycle
Psychological and Theological Perceptions

D0075011

Pre-publication
REVIEW

"This is a terrific book. Dayringer takes us back to childhood and moves us through time, providing fresh new insights into each stage of life. It will make you better understand where you are in life, why you feel the way you do at different ages, and what transitions occur along the way. It will also give you insight into why others—family members in particular—behave the way they do at different ages, thereby increasing empathy and compassion so necessary for healing. This book is special because it emphasizes spiritual as well as psychological and physical development, interweaving the three brilliantly."

Harold G. Koenig, MD
Associate Professor
of Medicine and of Psychiatry,
Department of Psychology
and Behavioral Sciences,
Duke University Medical Center,
Durham, NC

Life Cycle
Psychological and Theological Perceptions

PREVIOUS BOOKS BY RICHARD DAYRINGER

Pastor and Patient (Editor)

God Cares for You

The Heart of Pastoral Counseling (The Haworth Press)

Dealing with Depression (Editor) (The Haworth Press)

Life Cycle
Psychological and Theological Perceptions

Richard Dayringer, ThD

The Haworth Pastoral Press
An Imprint of The Haworth Press, Inc.
New York • London • Oxford

Published by

The Haworth Pastoral Press, an imprint of The Haworth Press, Inc., 10 Alice Street, Binghamton, NY 13904-1580

Cover design by Marylouise E. Doyle.

Library of Congress Cataloging-in-Publication Data

Dayringer, Richard.
  Life cycle : psychological and theological perceptions / Richard Dayringer.
     p.   cm.
  Includes bibliographical references and index.
  ISBN 0-7890-0171-3 (hardcover : alk. paper)—ISBN 0-7890-0905-6 (pbk. : alk. paper)
    1. Life cycle, Human—Religious aspects—Christianity. 2. Developmental psychology—Religious aspects—Christianity. I. Title.
  BV4597.555D38 1999
  248.4—dc21   99-37919
                                                                                                        CIP

To those who have assisted in my development:
my parents, Joseph Allen and Sarah Marlin (Ruppert);
my siblings, James Allen, Edgar Joe, Judith Ann, and Nancy Jane;
my wife, Evelyn Janet (Hymer);
my children, Stephen Lee, David Carter, Deborah Evelyn,
Daniel Hymer, and James Ray;
and my ACPE Chaplain Supervisor, Myron C. Madden.

ABOUT THE AUTHOR

Richard Dayringer, ThD, is Adjunct Professor at the Oklahoma Health Science Center-Tulsa in the Department of Family Medicine and in the Bioethics Center and Editor of the *American Journal of Pastoral Counseling.* Dr. Dayringer is Professor Emeritus and former Director of Psychosocial Care in the Department of Medical Humanities and Professor and Chief of Behavioral Science in the Department of Family and Community Medicine at Southern Illinois University School of Medicine in Springfield. A pastoral psychotherapist for over thirty years, he was Director of the Department of Pastoral Care and Counseling at Baptist Memorial Hospital in Kansas City for ten years before joining the faculty at SIU School of Medicine in 1974. Dr. Dayringer also served as a pastor in Missouri, Kansas, and Louisiana prior to beginning his academic career. He has served as a consultant to various organizations, including the Department of Allied Health at the University of Texas Medical Branch, the Walter Reed Army Hospital Department of Pastoral Care, the American Correctional Chaplains Association, and the Cleveland Clinic. He has given countless international, national, and local lectures and workshops on topics such as ethical issues in medicine, depression, pastoral interventions for the bereaved, and the spiritual and psychosocial aspects of AIDS. Dr. Dayringer is a member of the American Academy of Religion, an Approved Supervisor in the American Association for Marriage and Family Therapy, a Diplomate in the American Association of Pastoral Counselors, and a Certified Sex Therapist in the American Association of Sex Educators, Counselors, and Therapists. He is also a Chaplain Supervisor in the Association for Clinical Pastoral Education and a Certified Hypnotist in the Society for Clinical Hypnosis. He has written four books, *Pastor and Patient* (Aronson, 1982), *God Cares for You* (Broadman, 1983, large print edition, Walker, 1985), *Dealing with Depression* (Haworth, 1995), and *The Heart of Pastoral Counseling* (Revised edition, Haworth, 1998) and is the author of over seventy journal articles in the fields of medicine and pastoral care and counseling.

CONTENTS

THE GOD OF ALL AGES

O God of my infancy,
The Age of Grace;
I thank you for the
Undemanding love
Which came to me
From my parents.

O God of my toddling years,
The Age of Works;
I thank you for the
Kind, firm teachings
On timeliness, orderliness, and cleanliness
Which came to me
From my parents.

O God of my venturing years,
The Age of Family Romance;
I thank you for the
Love generated in me
For my parent of the opposite sex,
And for the understanding
Of my parent of the same sex.

O God of my grade school years,
The Age of Friendships;
I thank you for the
Teachers and peers
Who broadened my perspectives
And taught me how to compete.

From Dayringer, R. (1983). *God Cares for You.* Nashville: Broadman Press, pp. 138-140; large print edition, New York: Walker Publishing.

O God of my puberty,
The Age of Discovery;
I thank you for the
Newfound importance of
A close friend,
And for the fearful
Changes in my body
Which signaled my identity.

O God of my adolescence,
The Age of Struggle;
I thank you for the
Opposite sex
And your help in my
Contention with my
Identity and independence.

O God of my young adulthood,
The Age of Adjustment;
I thank you for my
Physical and intellectual powers
And for your guidance
In my selection of
A vocation and a spouse.

O God of my middle adulthood,
The Age of Achievement;
I thank you for my
Family of both origin and progeny,
For the success I attained,
And for your assistance
Through the mid-life crisis.

O God of my later adulthood,
The Age of Conservation;
I thank you for my
Health and my memories,
And for your presence with me
In all of life
And in death.

Foreword

In this book, Richard Dayringer will take you back, back, and back. It is a trip that helps you get the good feeling that our times are in the hands of God. It is not written to help us change so much as it is to help us celebrate things as they are. No two of us had the same journey through the years of our lives. Yet our stories are enough alike that when we understand our own story, we can identify with all the others.

I find that most personality development theorists have an aim to change people from being as they are. You will not find such in Richard Dayringer. The best change that comes about in any of us is that which comes as a result of our being able to understand and accept more fully things as they are.

As a reader, you might choose to go first with the chapter that deals with where you are presently in the life cycle. If you are a parent, it just might help you to be a kinder, gentler "giant" in dealing with the little people entrusted to you long enough for them to catch on to that swirling world out there. To them, it is always an anxious thing to break that second set of umbilical attachments and move out into the freedom they so sorely want and so dreadfully fear. Night after night they surrender the battle and retreat under cover of darkness to the hiding place where all souls are rewound for a new day. And one day, we hope and pray, they will make it!

In the first trip back, Dayringer covers the struggles and stresses of the human person beginning at birth. He takes a psychodynamic look at what it means for a child to be lifted from nature and thrust into a socializing process. It reminds one of the words of Winston Churchill that "every generation has to civilize a group of savages, namely its children." The animal in each of us protests the firm, controlling and shaping hand of civility. It is rather easy to forget our own resistance to putting on the harness of culture. Certainly none of us can remember how many diapers it took before we finally used one of them as a white flag of surrender. Time and order were no part of life in the beginning. We would have nothing to do with such until the "giants" came at us with "put it here, not there; do it now, not then; and never on Sunday."

Dayringer sees the stages in the life cycle as a kind of sacred journey. He relates them well to biblical metaphor. For example, he calls the very earliest cycle "the age of grace," one in which very few demands are placed on the child. Next comes command and often demand, and this stage is called "works." It makes you glad that in reality Abraham came before Moses. So throughout the book the author finds a way to interlace physical and psychological growth with spiritual development. He is not one who believes all psychological theories are to be taken as full truth. Yet he finds much in psychology, sociology, philosophy, and the behavioral sciences that sheds light on Scripture.

On the second trip back, the author deals with family. The first trip rather assumed family, but that is not enough. The family acts as a kind of new placenta, giving growing persons much more space than they had in utero, and yet not the kind of space they will need as full-scale adults. Dynamic psychology did not apply its insights to the human family until it first studied the individual person. Studying the person in the family brings new appreciation for the creative hand of God at work in both nature and history.

The third trip through the life cycle is the author's attempt to make new meaning of the various theories that help us relate to our growth and development as human beings. That growth and development may be interpreted only as a secular story. It becomes a sacred journey when we look at it with the faith that divine purpose is guiding the process.

Having known Richard Dayringer over the years, I have seen him in the struggle and search for knowledge and insight about us as human beings. But what is splendid about him is a humility that guides his journey, a journey of faith in which he and his lovely wife, Janet, have lived together from late adolescence to retirement.

Myron C. Madden, PhD
ACPE Chaplain Supervisor
AAPC Diplomate

All the world's a stage,
And all the men and women merely players:
They have their exits and their entrances;
And one man in his time plays many parts,
His acts being seven ages. At first the infant,
Mewling and puking in the nurse's arms.
And then the whining schoolboy, with his satchel
And shining morning face, creeping like snail
Unwillingly to school. And then the lover,
Sighing like furnace, with a woeful ballad
Made to his mistress' eyebrow. Then a soldier,
Full of strange oaths and bearded like the pard,
Jealous in honor, sudden and quick in quarrel,
Seeking the bubble reputation
Even in the cannon's mouth. And then the justice,
In fair round belly with good capon lined,
With eyes severe and beard of formal cut,
Full of wise saws and modern instances;
And so he plays his part. The sixth age shifts
Into the lean and slipper'd pantaloon,
With spectacles on nose and pouch on side,
His youthful hose, well saved, a world too wide
For his shrunk shank; and his big manly voice,
Turning again toward childish treble, pipes
And whistles in his sound. Last scene of all,
That ends this strange eventful history,
Is second childishness and mere oblivion,
Sans teeth, sans eyes, sans taste, sans everything.

Shakespeare
As You Like It
Act II, scene vii

Introduction

The life cycle has intrigued me since, as a youngster, I was encouraged by a wide range of people in a variety of ways to "get big." My first source has, obviously, been the sixty-five-year study of one person—myself. As Henry David Thoreau wrote in *Walden:* "I should not talk so much about myself if there were anybody else whom I knew as well."

The second primary source that I have studied has been (like Piaget, 1970, 1977) our own five children and now eleven grandchildren. The third primary source has been the more than 1,000 counselees with whom I worked in longer-term pastoral psychotherapy, along with the extensive notes I have kept. These people have shared the development of their lives in intense and intimate dimensions. We typically took the time to allow them to unfold their memories from the earliest, moving year to year, grade to grade, residence to residence, and including as many of their relationships with people as possible.

The secondary sources include the entries listed in the bibliography of this book. The teacher who influenced me most in this area was the Reverend Myron C. Madden, PhD, who has written the foreword. He was my Chaplain Supervisor in Clinical Pastoral Education at the Southern Baptist Hospital in New Orleans. I want to acknowledge my indebtedness to him for much of the material in Chapters 3, 4, and 5.

I have been teaching this material yearly since 1965 to a large number of rather widely diverse students in clinical pastoral education, seminary, medicine, and also family practice residents. Their feedback has definitely challenged and refined these ideas.

My assumption that normal human growth and development proceeds in stages has been posited as a truism without offering philosophical arguments for its accuracy. The age range of each stage is rather arbitrary, but individuals do "customize" their lives. The natural process of development threatens past accomplishments and disrupts stability. It includes the notions of improvement, fulfillment, and completion. Theologically (Whitehead, 1992, p. 14), we must remember that "God gave the growth" (1 Cor. 3:6).

The purpose of this book is to trace personality development with one eye on psychological findings and the other on theological understandings with the hope that both eyes may see a new vision. I believe that those who want to help people, whether in the profession of medicine or ministry, must clearly understand the stage of life the person to be helped is in and the most likely stage of the life cycle wherein the problem originated. My fear is that too little attention is given to these issues. I agree with the Levinsons (1996) that the "primary components of a life structure are the person's *relationships* with various others in the external world" (p. 22; cf. Dayringer, 1998).

When I compare and contrast my studies of the life cycle from the 1960s to the turn of the century, I agree with Gail Sheehy's concept (1995, p. 5) that there has been a ten-year shift forward in the stages from adolescence and beyond. I also admire her attempt to put generations into five cohorts (p. 25) according to their time of birth. However, I have not attempted to do that in my work. Keeping up with the research in this discipline has been difficult and has called for annual revisions. For this reason, I have found it difficult to release this manuscript to the publisher, but perhaps now is as good a time as any.

I want to thank my colleagues in the Department of Medical Humanities at the Southern Illinois University School of Medicine for their assistance in the annual teaching of the course "What's Normal in Human Growth and Development" and also those faculty members and residents who assisted from the departments of family medicine, pediatrics, and psychiatry.

I also want to thank Peg Marr of The Haworth Press. Her editorial assistance was invaluable.

Chapter 1

The Age of Adjustment:
Twenty to Forty Years

One of the best places to begin studying the family life cycle according to the family systems theory (Capps, 1983; Carter and McGoldrick, 1988) of human development is with a marriage and the creation of a family. For most people, this happens during young adulthood. Robert Kegan (1982), a psychologist, characterizes the self during this stage of life, when individuals are claiming to author their own lives, as the institutional self. Obviously, much is yet to be learned about the struggle to achieve adulthood. I call this stage of life the age of adjustment.

Actually, only a little interest has been shown in adult development until quite recently. This is in spite of the fact that we spend only one-third of our lives growing up and two-thirds of them growing old, being adults.

When I was a doctoral student at New Orleans Baptist Theological Seminary beginning in 1961, there was a course taught by Dr. Donald Minton titled "The Psychology of Adulthood." He was just starting to teach this new course and I was his teaching assistant. He and I dug like mad to find anything on the subject in the library. The seminary has a huge library but there was little to be found about adult development. Erik H. Erikson (1903-1994), with his publication of *Childhood and Society* in 1950, was the most influential developmental theorist of the time. One psychologist said the lack of interest in adulthood is because of the dread of middle age. Psychologists had not yet become interested in exploring this area. Fortunately, much more interest has been shown recently.

Let me mention three authors among the scores who have written on this topic. The best known is Gail Sheehy. She has been widely read since *Passages* was first published in 1974. In fact, it was on the best-seller list for a long time. Many people have read two of her other books (Sheehy, 1995, 1998), especially people approaching middle age. But she has much to say to adults throughout the range of adulthood. Sheehy is not a psychologist; she is simply a journalist who has gathered a lot of material from others who have studied adult development. She has pulled together the available knowledge and put it in a nice, readable package.

The second author is Roger Gould, a psychiatrist who wrote a book titled *Transformations* (1978). The third author is a psychologist, Daniel Levinson, who along with his research associates wrote *The Seasons of a Man's Life* (Levinson et al., 1978) and *The Seasons of a Woman's Life* (Levinson and Levinson, 1996).

THE SEASONS OF A MAN'S LIFE

Dr. Levinson was a professor of psychology in the Department of Psychiatry at the Yale School of Medicine. When he went there he decided to study adulthood, got a research grant, and pulled a team of scholars together. He selected a group of forty male subjects very carefully. The forty men fell into four vocational groups of ten each. There were ten biologists, ten novelists, ten workers or wage earners, and ten executives. Fifteen percent of the forty were rural and urban poor. Forty-two percent were working lower middle class. Thirty-two percent were middle class and ten percent were the wealthiest class. The subjects were between the ages of thirty-five and forty-five when he began his study. He has followed them through the years and interviewed them regularly, from time to time, as they grew older. Thus, he tried to select forty men who represented all men in society (see Figure 1.1). Later he and his wife, Judy, selected fifteen business women, fifteen female faculty members, and fifteen homemakers for their study of the seasons of a woman's life (Levinson and Levinson, 1996, pp. 201, 202).

What Levinson calls the "novice" period roughly corresponds to the age group that I cover in this chapter and call the age of adjustment. It has three distinct periods. He calls ages seventeen to twenty-two the "Early Adult Transition." Roger Gould, in his book *Transformations* (1978), suggests that people develop and rely on a

FIGURE 1.1. The Seasons of a Man's Life

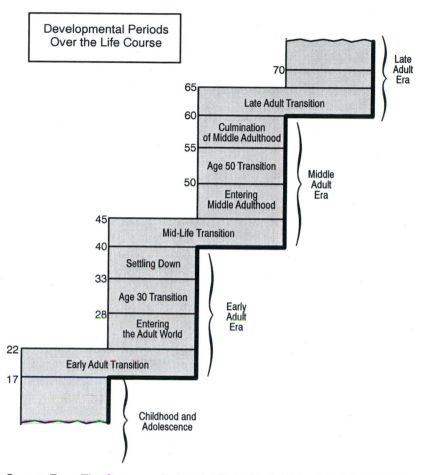

kind of slogan to get through each age bracket. For people in this period, the typical slogan is "my parents can guarantee my safety." Young people do seem to live that way: "I really don't have to worry; my parents will get me out of jail; they'll get me in another college; they'll get me a loan; they'll pay off my bills," and so on.

The second of these novice phases is ages twenty-two to twenty-eight, which Levinson calls "Entering the Adult World." Gould says that the slogan or myth for people in this age group is, "I'm nobody's baby now" and "a spouse will guarantee happiness." The shift in dependence now is from the parent to the spouse.

The last of these age brackets is twenty-eight to thirty-three. Levinson calls this the "Age Thirty Transition." Gould's slogan is, "Life is a simple, manageable proposition" (I can handle it). This slogan indicates less dependency on someone else but still an unrealistic view of life, which is not all that simple and not that easy to manage.

During this entire novice stage there are four developmental tasks, which Levinson discovered by interviewing his subjects. The first of these is the process of forming a dream. His male subjects began to form a dream concerning what they wanted to do with their lives. Several of them were pushed back from their dreams by their circumstances. Their parents might have said, "Look, you could never get accepted into a veterinary school because of your grades." Or parents might have said to a young man who wants to get a doctorate and teach in a university, "We don't have that kind of money; that is too many years." The high school counselor and math teachers may tell a young man they really don't think he has the capability to become an engineer. Some have to abandon the dream or alter it.

On the other hand, an individual may be pushed toward a dream that actually belongs to the parents. This is most common among farmers and physicians. If Dad is a farmer or physician, the son is (statistically) most likely to follow in his footsteps. It happens in all vocations sometimes. Some men get into careers that do not hold any personal interest for them. Jobs have a way of locking a person in with increasing wages or salaries, growing benefits including retirement, and seniority. It is an awfully big choice to decide to bail out.

Levinson found among his subjects that the people who were able to build their lives around their dreams had a much better chance for happiness, satisfaction, and self-fulfillment than the ones who, for one reason or another, could not or would not pursue their dreams.

The second developmental task Levinson found among his subjects was the formation of a mentor relationship. A mentor is a person who will support and facilitate the realization of the dream. A mentor is a kind of mixture of a parent and a peer. The mentor relationship may develop at the work setting in the person of a boss or senior colleague, someone who has been on the job for awhile. It can develop in a graduate or professional school situation with a senior faculty member. The mentor gives the younger man "a leg up" in climbing the professional ladder. Young ministers usually refer to some older minister with more experience as their "father in the ministry." The older minister takes an interest in the younger minister and may, for instance, write letters of reference, supervise counseling, advise concerning church problems, and so forth. It works similarly in any vocation. The mentor is a great deal of help in enabling the younger person to get ahead in his vocation or to show what he can do.

The relationship with the mentor lasts on the average from perhaps as little as two to three years to as many as eight to ten years. Finally it does come to an end. It may end because one of the two moves away or dies. It may end because of a conflict between the two. This typically occurs because the younger person wants to push ahead with a new idea and the mentor is not supportive of it, so the two disagree and part company. The mentor is quite important in helping a young person to launch a career.

Josef Breuer served as a mentor for Sigmund Freud. Breuer was fourteen years older than Freud and well established and respected in medicine. He was extremely generous in making loans to Freud, which eventually reached a staggering total of 2,300 gulden. Breuer was an intellectual patron to Freud as well. He introduced Freud to the case of Fraulein Anna O. and the cathartic method or talking cure. Freud eventually persuaded Breuer to collaborate with him on their book, *Studies on Hysteria* (Breuer and Freud, 1936). Freud seemed to be primarily responsible for ending their mentorship because Breuer disagreed with his claim of a sexual etiology for all neuroses. Breuer's daughter-in-law told a story of walking with Breuer and seeing Freud approaching. She said Breuer instinctively opened his arms but Freud passed by, pretending not to see him (Oring, 1997, *The Jokes of Sigmund Freud*).

In my case, my father in the ministry also became my father-in-law. He was my pastor and he gave me opportunities to preach. The church sponsored a weekly service at the local county jail and I preached there often. He talked to the associational Director of Missions about me and recommended me to the Mentor Baptist Church near Springfield, Missouri, which became my first pastorate. More often than not, there is a mentor for the person who fulfills his or her dream.

Forming a vocation is the third developmental task discussed by Levinson. Choosing a vocation is too narrow a concept. In my own experience, I chose the ministry and at the time the only thing I knew about the ministry was the pastorate. As the years have gone by, I have functioned in a number of areas within the ministry. During my college years I was interested in evangelism. I served as a pastor while studying for the master of divinity degree. During my doctoral studies, I became interested in chaplaincy, counseling, and teaching. When I finished my resident studies at the seminary, I had two opportunities: a pastorate and a chaplaincy position. I chose the latter out of a conviction of stewardship: others were as well prepared as I to serve the pastorate, but I had been privileged to accumulate specialized training for the chaplaincy and to begin a program of clinical pastoral education. So, I accepted the position as director of the Department of Pastoral Care and Counseling at Baptist Memorial Hospital in Kansas City. Ten years later, with the same conviction, I accepted an invitation to teach in the two Departments of Medical Humanities and Family Practice at Southern Illinois University School of Medicine. It was a progressive, innovative school, and I was one of the first ministers hired as a full-time faculty member by a medical school. At the time I entered my vocation, this sort of thing was unheard of. When I first set my foot on the road to ministry, I had no notion about what I ultimately would come to do. Nearly any vocation, once a person develops it, is much broader than previously thought.

The mentor phenomenon is quite different for women since fewer mentors are available for them. Female mentors used to be particularly scarce, but recently their numbers have increased. When a man takes an interest in advising and guiding a young woman, there is often an erotic interest as well, which complicates the relationship.

Margaret Hennig in her Harvard doctoral dissertation (1970), studied twenty-five high-level women executives. She found 100 women presidents and vice presidents of large corporations listed in *Who's Who in America*. All had a strong attachment to a particular male boss early in their careers. She selected twenty-five of these women and traced their lives stage by stage. Each one was a first-born in her family. Around age twenty-five they all decided to put their careers ahead of marriage and a family. For the next thirty years they remained with the same firms and were promoted along with their mentors. Around age thirty-five all of them took a moratorium for a year or two. They took a long, hard look at themselves and their goals. Almost half of them married professional men during this time.

Dr. Hennig also selected a control group who got stuck in middle management and compared their characteristics with her study group. She noted that the fathers of the women in the control group treated their daughters exactly as though they were sons, even calling them boy's names. These women formed only "buddy" relationships with bosses. They did not take a mid-thirties moratorium to reevaluate their lives. None married. They did not get promoted to the top.

The fourth developmental task Levinson found in the lives of his male subjects was that of finding a special woman. The young man with a dream found a special woman who would help him pursue that dream. This special woman was like a mentor in some ways and could, in fact, even be the mentor, but that was not often the case. She supported the young man emotionally as he pursued his dream and may even have supported him financially. This special woman was not necessarily his wife, but usually was his wife. She might have been a teacher or a close friend. For some men she was an older guide, critic, or sponsor. For the novelists, she was sometimes a financial sponsor who would contribute money to give the man time to write. The special woman for some of these men was a transitional figure, especially if she was not the wife. Among professionals, wives supported the men until "liftoff" (the obtaining of the professional degree), but then were soon dropped (often divorced) like the first stage of a space rocket. But the special woman was a very important figure who helped enable the man to fulfill his dream. This is the way that men get started in adult life.

WOMEN'S LIFESTYLES

That is not the trend for women, who create their adult lives in a different way. Gail Sheehy in *Passages* (pp. 293-347) describes six life patterns for women. She talks about women who become *caregivers*. Before this century most women gave a priority to caregiving. This is still the choice of many young women. They find a man to love, bear children, and raise and care for them.

Other women choose the lifestyle of a *nurturer who defers personal achievement*. This is somewhat different. These women choose first of all to be caregivers or nurturers, but they keep in mind during marriage and child rearing that later they want careers of their own. These women begin college and may finish their degree and even work for a year or two. But they set aside careers to marry and have children, fully planning to resume their professions after the children have started school or left home. These women dedicate seven to twenty-five years toward helping their children advance their lives, while keeping their personal career goals and achievement in mind. They simply give nurturing the priority in their lives. These are the women who go back to school in midlife. Nursing schools often prefer to accept women in this age group over younger women. Nursing facilities invest a lot of energy into young women, many of whom are nurturers who defer achievement and drop out of nursing soon after they graduate. Older nurturers who defer achievement go to work after graduation and work without interruption for the next twenty-five years.

A third lifestyle for women is the *achiever who defers nurturing*. These women postpone marriage and motherhood to spend six to ten years completing their professional preparation and establishing themselves in careers. These women definitely plan to get into nurturing later in life. Around age thirty, before losing the physiological ability to bear children, these women declare a moratorium in their careers and give nurturing the priority. Some women in this category are super-achievers such as Margaret Mead, the sociologist who established a wide reputation for herself as an anthropologist and then had her children. Barbara Walters of television fame and actress Sophia Loren are other examples.

Another lifestyle for women is the *integrator:* these women, from the first, plan to combine both nurturing and achievement at the same time. This is a very difficult thing to do, and yet some women seem able to attain it. The main problem may be finding the physical and mental energy to accomplish this lifestyle. I think that women who select this option, thinking it will mean "having it all," may be frequently plagued by guilt—that they cannot devote time and energy fully to either family or job.

Society seems to have designated only one lifestyle for men: the achiever who defers nurturing. Some men have insisted on a choice and have selected the style of the integrator. Many women wish more men would choose to be integrators.

The fifth lifestyle is *never married women.* About 10 percent of women never marry. That makes them slightly different from the achiever who puts off nurturing. They start out as achievers but never get around to nurturing. For some of these it is by choice but for others it is simply circumstantial. I suspect we all know women in both categories.

The last lifestyle is *transient women,* who wander from job to job and perhaps from man to man. This is a very small percentage of women who do not appear to have any particular plans for their lives. They are not really interested in achieving or nurturing.

TYPICAL CHARACTERISTICS

Some characteristics are typical of adulthood during the age of adjustment from ages twenty to thirty-five. The physical powers among these young people mature so that physically they are about as strong as they ever have been or ever will be. Most of the Olympic champions are in their twenties. The big exception to that is the young girls who win swimming and gymnastics medals, may be below the age of twenty. But almost all of us have our greatest athletic skill and ability during our twenties. We are active and vigorous and we have great endurance.

Intellectually, people in the age of adjustment are also at the height of their powers. Vigorous intellectual growth is going on during this time. They are beginning to attain some of their goals, such as graduating from college, starting a career, getting married, and having children. So they extend their goals or set them higher. This is the age group in which the highest earned academic degree is often achieved. They usually complete their formal education pursuits in this period. At least they think they have; later on in midlife they might decide to go back to school, but usually they think they have all the formal education they want at this time in life. Young people in college can still learn things rapidly. Learning ability continues until approximately age twenty-four and then only declines 1 percent yearly.

By their mid- to late twenties, young people begin to realize that they have accumulated a greater breadth of knowledge than ever and that they are becoming intellectually experienced. They often value their own opinions based on their aggregate of information as much or more than the opinions of parents, bosses, or other authority figures.

Robert Havighurst, in his book *Developmental Tasks and Education* (1972), lists nine developmental tasks for early adulthood. Table 1.1 lists my understanding of developmental tasks in young adulthood. I will use these as something of an outline for the remainder of this chapter.

TABLE 1.1. The Challenges of the Age of Adjustment

Perplexities/Pains_____Growth/Gains

Completing identity

Leaving home

Finishing education

Moving into a vocation

Finding a congenial social group

Confirming values and beliefs

Forming an intimate relationship

Starting a family

Managing a home

Rearing children

Balancing time for self, family, job

Taking a civic responsibility

Jesus, as a young adult, was faced with the question of his identity. In the beginning of his public ministry, at his baptism, John the Baptist tried to deter him (Matt. 3:14,15). A couple of years later, he asked his disciples, "Who do people say that I am? . . . Who do you say that I am?" (Mark 8:27, 29). We get some of our identity from making a vocational choice. This is true of both men and women but historically more so of men. Individuals are called by job titles: mail carrier, pastor, nurse, secretary. The Protestant work ethic and the success syndrome in modern, Western countries has had a great impact and has motivated people to merge their personalities with their jobs as a way of firming up their identity. In earlier times, each occupation had its own unique hat or even uniform that each worker wore so that a baker, sailor, chauffeur, etc., could be easily recognized.

The process of leaving home takes a long time for some individuals. According to a Census Bureau report, 15 percent of males and 8 percent of females between twenty-five and thirty-four who had never married still lived with their parents in 1990 and 1995 (Brunner, 1997, p. 365).

One of the developmental tasks is moving into a vocation. Having already chosen and prepared for an occupation, the age of adjustment is the time to get started. Freud was once asked what he thought a normal person should be able to do well. "Lieben und arbeiten," he said: to love and to work.

People often don't enjoy their work. Professional people rate the nature of their work as their greatest single source of satisfaction, but industrial workers emphasize pay rates and fringe benefits as most important in their work. Professional people tend to find much satisfaction in their work and spend a lot of time doing it. Wage earners tend to find much less satisfaction in the work that they do and more satisfaction in the time outside the work hours. The best part of the working day for the wage earner often is the time at the plant before the whistle blows to start work, during the lunch hour, or immediately after work. They work to earn money so they can do what they want after work and on the weekends. Wage earners may spend more time with their families than professionals. Professional people tend to like their jobs so much that they may take work home. These are the professionals who go to the office on Saturday and may neglect their family as a result.

Another developmental task for persons in the age of adjustment is to confirm one's values and beliefs. Fowler (1987, pp. 68-71) named the religious development that occurs during this stage of life individuative reflective faith. Beliefs are reexamined on the basis of personal knowledge and experience. This raises questions such as, Where do I pledge my allegiance? How can I follow the instruction of the Apostle Paul to make my "manner of life be worthy of the gospel of Christ" (Phil. 1:27)? Do I perceive a divine purpose for my life?

Another developmental task for those in the age of adjustment is forming an intimate relationship. For many men, the difficulty with intimacy revolves around the word *connection*. Men wonder how they can draw close to others in ways that will not threaten their sense of independence. Women often feel tense about *separation*. They wonder how they nourish personal autonomy in ways that do not diminish the important connections they have with other people (Whitehead, 1992, p. 7).

Dating, of course, begins during the teenage years. Some even marry then, as did my wife and I. Young adults date more and more frequently as they develop a feeling of comfort with the opposite sex. They also compare different dating partners until they build an image of their ideal mate. This ideal mate usually has some unconscious reference to the parent of the opposite gender, similar or dissimilar. "Going steady" is a culturally approved reciprocal agreement between a man and woman to exclude all possible dating partners except each other in order to experiment with marital fidelity. This enables the pair to get to know each other in much greater depth.

Premarital sexual intercourse is quite common in modern America and even more so since the advent of the birth control pill, which was developed by Roman Catholic physician John Rock and was approved in this country in 1960. The Church teaching about sexual abstinence before marriage has been heeded less and less. The number of couples living together without the blessing of marriage tripled in the United States between the censuses of 1970 and 1980. One-fourth of these unmarried couples have children living with them. The sociologists concluded that those couples who cohabitate before marriage are more likely to divorce because they are less committed to marriage and more accepting of divorce (Axinn and Thornton, 1992). Nonetheless, 90 percent of Americans will marry at least once.

Only a firm sense of personal and sexual identity enables one to relate intimately to another person in a marital relationship. The lack of adequate identity is one of the reasons for the failure of many marriages. Marriage is used by many young people as a status-achieving device. It is a way to get status, a way to get out of the parental home, and a way to be recognized as an adult.

People marry for many reasons; love is just one of them. They also marry for economic security, because they desire a home, because they want children, for emotional security, because of their parents' wishes, to escape loneliness, to escape their parental home, for companionship, because of sexual attraction, for protection, to gain notoriety, to gain social position, because of gratitude, to gain citizenship ("green card"), for spite, to gain pity, for adventure, because of common interests, because of a wish to conform, or for the satisfaction of ego needs.

Several studies over the years have attempted to isolate predictors of marital happiness. The following factors have usually surfaced in this research:

1. Positive personality traits such as optimism
2. Similarity of cultural backgrounds
3. Socially responsive personalities
4. Harmonious family environments
5. Compatible religious backgrounds
6. Satisfying occupations
7. A love relationship
8. Wholesome attitudes toward sexual relations

The average age at the time of the first marriage according to the 1970 census was 20.8 for women and 23.2 for men; in 1980 it was 22.1 for women and 24.6 for men; in 1990, 24 and 26 respectively. Thus, the current trend is for young adults to put off marriage longer than did their parents. According to a recent Census Bureau report, people are now older at the time of their first marriage than at any time in the bureau's 100-year history (Associated Press, 1991). Still, they are not happy about remaining single for so long. Single women were especially bothered by a study which appeared in

Newsweek on June 2, 1986 (Salholz, 1986). The findings reported were that white, college-educated women who were still single at age thirty have only a 20 percent chance of ever marrying. By thirty-five, the odds drop to 5 percent. Forty-year-old women are more likely to be killed by a terrorist than to marry. They have a minuscule 2.6 percent probability of marriage.

After selecting a marriage partner, newlyweds have ahead of them the arduous task of learning to live together. That is not always easy. Frequently this occurs during the completion of formal educational pursuits. Until World War II, young adults generally delayed marriage until education was complete, but by the early 1960s, approximately 20 percent of undergraduates and half of graduate students were married. This trend is still increasing, but there are some disadvantages to being married while still in school. The student spouse may also be a working spouse who is thus caught in a double bind of trying to keep up with studies and a job. Both lower grades and a poorer job performance may be the result. Student spouses may feel guilty for letting their spouses support them if they do not work or because of neglecting their children to study. The working spouse may develop resentment toward the student spouse who does not work or help much with household chores in order to study. And, the student spouse may "outgrow" the working spouse intellectually, giving the couple less common knowledge to discuss. Then there is pregnancy, which almost always causes the student wife to drop out of school. Yet, in spite of these disadvantages, Rachel Cox found in her study of fifty-two couples who married in their undergraduate years, which she reported in her book titled *Youth into Maturity* (1970), that with few exceptions the strength and satisfaction of these marriages increased during the ten years of her study.

People expect intimacy in a marriage relationship, but many have a one-dimensional view of intimacy as merely sexual. Sexual intimacy provides erotic or orgasmic closeness, and I will discuss it more fully later. Intimacy also has a number of other dimensions. Howard and Charlotte Clinebell have done an excellent job of summarizing these dimensions in their book *The Intimate Marriage* (1970) as has Muriel James in her book *Marriage Is for Loving* (1979).

Emotional intimacy involves being tuned to each other's emotional wavelengths and sharing such feelings as love, joy, or sadness. Intellectual intimacy includes sharing the world of great ideas. It thrives in an atmosphere of freedom where spouses can express differences of opinion without fear of being ridiculed. Aesthetic intimacy shares experiences of beauty such as looking at a moonlit lake or a painting. Creative intimacy occurs when couples do something together such as landscaping the yard, decorating the house, or making handicrafts. Creating children is a part of this as well. Recreational intimacy occurs when couples relate in experiences of fun and play. The problem with some attempts at recreational intimacy is that couples get into competition with each other and spoil it. Work intimacy is closeness in sharing common tasks such as cleaning the house or taking care of the yard. Crisis intimacy involves closeness in coping with problems and pain. Some families in the middle of a terrible sickness or accident genuinely support one another. Commitment intimacy is mutually derived from joint self-investment in each other or a common belief such as Christianity. Conflict intimacy involves facing and struggling with differences honestly and openly. There should be room for more than one opinion in any marriage. Spiritual intimacy is the "We-ness" in sharing ultimate concerns. Communication intimacy embraces the source of all types of true intimacy and leads to a lifelong conversation. Women: learn to laugh. Give your family a happy spouse and mother. Men: learn to talk. Let your family know what you think and how you feel.

It would be wonderful if all of us shared each of those kinds of intimacies frequently—and we would if it were not for the barriers to intimacy. (The Clinebells [Clinebell and Clinebell, 1970] and Muriel James [1979] also have good sections on these topics.) Emotional immaturity gets in the way of intimacy in young marriages but it certainly is not relegated only to the young. Emotional immaturity takes many forms in marriage, such as maintaining a primary commitment to parents, acting as though still single, expecting to get instead of to give and receive, demanding to be made happy, wanting to be taken care of, or showing little control of impulses (such as handling credit cards or sexual impulses).

Inadequate personal identity is another barrier. If I do not know who I am, it is hard for me to relate to someone else intimately. If I expect my spouse to tell me who I am, then I do not have much of significance to give. This is one of the reasons for the failure of so many teenage marriages.

Some couples avoid closeness because one of them is afraid of getting hurt. Many people have been hurt in a previous love relationship. Intimacy involves constant vulnerability to the possibility of being hurt.

Low self-esteem is another barrier. If you do not feel worthy of being loved, it is difficult to believe that your spouse loves you.

Guilt is a barrier to intimacy. Regret over some misdeed in the past makes one feel unworthy of love.

Substitution of counterfeit intimacy for the real thing is a barrier. This may involve manipulation or lead to impersonal sexual intercourse. The reason for this may be that one spouse is unwilling or unable to enter an in-depth relationship.

Chronic busyness detracts from intimacy because the latter takes time to develop. The workaholic or the person who is focused on material things will seldom have the patience to just enjoy being with the loved one.

Mishandled hostility, anger, or resentment get in the way of intimacy. Hostility is inevitable in marriage and should be admitted, expressed, and worked through. George Bach has numerous suggestions for handling anger creatively in his book, *The Intimate Enemy* (Bach and Wyden, 1969).

We all attempt to manipulate our spouses. Some of us are good at it and make them like it, or subtle enough to keep the spouse from even noticing it. Others are not skilled and make their spouses angry.

One spouse treating the other as a parent is a frequent block to marital intimacy. Carl Jung (1971) maintained that people project the image of both good and bad parenting onto their partners. Persistently addressing your spouse by a parental name such as Mom or Dad may be a sign of this. It leads you to expect the spouse to do all sorts of things for you. You may get angry if your spouse doesn't draw your bath water, shine your shoes, or lay out your clothes. Remember, though, that sleeping with a "parent" is hard on your sex life.

Competition between the spouses inhibits intimacy. Vying for control of the budget, kids, or sex may feel like the rivalry experienced with siblings in growing up. In traditional marriages, the man was the head of the house, and the woman was the heart. Nowadays, equality may foster competition.

Marital games, according to Eric Berne in his book *Games People Play* (1967), are interpersonal transactions in which each person has an ulterior motive. These emotional games, such as "mine is better than yours" or "see what you made me do," help couples to avoid intimacy.

One last barrier to marital intimacy is disagreement over the female and male role expectations. These role images come from the families who raised us and lead us to expect each gender to do certain work and behave in particular ways.

Having dealt with the varieties of intimacy and the barriers to intimacy, let me say a few more things about sexual intimacy. Many people agree that sex is the most pleasurable and fun-filled dimension of intimacy. Someone has said that only two kinds of people exist: those who are interested in sex, and liars. It may have been Johnny Carson who said that sex takes the least time and causes the most trouble. Erik Erikson wrote concerning young adulthood in his book *Childhood and Society* (1963, p. 76) "It is only now that true gentility can fully develop."

The Church has often been accused of teaching that the only purpose for sex is reproduction. But neither the Church nor the Bible has denied that there are also other purposes for sex. It provides a physical means for the expression of love and the unification of the marital couple. It certainly provides the couple with a means of enjoyment and pleasure. And it strengthens each spouse's personal sexual identity. The Reverend Jeremy Taylor, a sixteenth-century Anglican priest, was one of the first in theological literature to list the purposes of marital coitus in his book, *The Rule and Exercises of Holy Living* (Taylor, 1982). He included the following reasons: a desire for children, to avoid fornication, to lighten and ease the cares and sadness of household living, and to endear each other.

Another of the developmental tasks for some people during the age of adjustment is learning to live alone. Ten percent of the people in our country never marry. And less than 10 percent choose a lifestyle of homosexuality.

Some people marry and start to live together but then divorce. The average length of the first marriage for those who divorce is seven years. Of course, divorce has become more acceptable in our society. The currently divorced population has more than quadrupled, from 4.3 million in 1970 to 18.3 million in 1996. They represented 10 percent of adults age eighteen and above in 1996, up from 3 percent in 1970 (Brunner, 1998, p. 351). There are now three peaks in the divorce scale for this country. The highest is around age thirty. The next highest is during the forties, when the kids are teenagers, and the newest and lowest peak is during the sixties, following retirement. On average, five out of six divorced men will remarry and three out of four divorced women will remarry. For instance, examine these statistics:

- Of men still unmarried at age thirty, 70 percent will marry.
- Of women still single at age thirty, 55 percent will marry before age fifty.
- Of those still single at thirty-five, half of the men and one-third of the women will marry.
- By age forty, the men's chance of marriage is 1 in 4, the women's 1 in 6 (Kaluger and Kaluger, 1974, p. 258).

Interesting things have happened to married men and women by the time they get well into their thirties. A major longitudinal study at The Institute of Human Development at The University of California in Berkeley (Block and Haan, 1971) compared the experiences of men and women who were married and in their thirties. They found that men had increased confidence and greater social control. They felt more dependable, more productive, more assertive, more independent, more capable of giving advice, more satisfied with themselves, more aware of their social powers, and more aware of their sexual powers. They were aware of some loss of tenderness and self-expression.

Women, on the other hand, felt less sure of themselves. They felt more submissive, more fearful, more guilty, more controlled, more hostile, more protective, more introspective, and more sympathetic.

Sexual enjoyment had declined for them and they felt secure only in their role as mother.

Along similar lines, Carol Gilligan, in her book *In a Different Voice* (1982, p. 42), found that men see in intimate relationships a danger of entrapment or betrayal, being smothered, or humiliated by rejection and deceit. In contrast, women fear the lack of intimacy: isolation. They are afraid that vocational achievement, standing out, or being set apart by success will cause them to be left alone.

Research studies show that in general, in our culture, the presence of a religious faith is associated with more favorable chances of marital success. Studies reported by the Landises in their book *Building a Successful Marriage* (Landis and Landis, 1963, pp. 351, 352), covering approximately 25,000 marriages, have shown that there were three times as many marital failures among people with no religious affiliation as among those belonging to a given religion.

Starting a family is another developmental task for young adults. Some get married and never start a family because of biological problems or personal choice. In general, young people are putting off starting a family until later in life than they used to. The average age of the woman at the birth of her first child is greater now than it used to be. First births to women twenty-five and older more than doubled in the dozen years after 1970. Among women thirty to thirty-four, first births tripled in these twelve years (Baldwin and Nord, 1984). Because birth control devices are better, couples have more choice than they used to about when to start a family. Roughly 400 times in the life of a woman, she must decide whether or not to leave herself open to pregnancy. In other words, in a lifetime her body will produce about 400 ova that could become fertilized.

There used to be a saying that a child was good for a marriage. In fact, girls are taught, especially in magazines, movies, and novels, to believe the myth that marriage and children will always bring happiness. We know now that this is not true; a child puts more stress on a marriage. Therefore, the parents ought to be stabilized in their relationship as much as possible before the first child arrives. We also know that a great percentage of people marry when the wife is already pregnant. Their child will come before the parents can get ready emotionally. Young people who marry at twenty and have a baby at twenty-one, for example, have little time to develop independent identities or even the potential for intimacy between husband and wife.

During a marriage the periods of pregnancy are times of expectancy and anxiety. Pregnancy stirs up the fear of death during childbirth. It may also arouse unresolved oedipal feelings (see Chapter 4) in either spouse and a beginning of competition with the new baby for the spouse's love.

Once a baby is born, it certainly imposes new strains on husband-wife intimacy. They will each share a feeling of responsibility for this new life. Both spouses will sleep less and experience more fatigue. The baby will demand a percentage of time from each spouse that will cut into time they formerly had for each other. And, strange as it may seem, one of the two parents is likely to have to deal with some personal feelings of jealousy toward the baby. The love and attention that one spouse lavishes on the baby will cause the other spouse to wonder if he or she has fallen into second place. A little periodic reassurance can do wonders to reduce this very real problem. The Levinsons (1996, pp. 43, 44) concluded that a mother who gives care to her baby also receives care in three ways: (1) directly from bonding with her infant, (2) by "re-mothering" herself, and (3) from her husband.

Rearing children once you have them is the next developmental task on our list. This is something that nobody is equipped to do automatically, and yet few of us do much directly to prepare ourselves for being a parent. Probably the best thing to read is *P.E.T: Parent Effectiveness Training* (Gordon, 1975). Courses in parent effectiveness training are available, and I think churches should do young parents a real favor by offering these courses now and again. Or, courses could be taught periodically on parenting children in each age range during the life cycle. One of the best things to do for parents is simply to offer them a chance to get together in interest groups and talk about what they do and what works. People sharing ideas can learn a lot without any expert present.

On the average, children will not reach adolescence, and probably not even puberty, while their parents are in the age of adjustment. Still, ten years of parenting forces young adults to assume more and more of the adult role. Many of them will continue to wonder throughout these years why they do not feel as sure and confident as their parents seemed to be.

The good parent does not say much about the sacrifices made for the child but does tell each child often about the love felt for her or him. The parent does not attempt to maintain the absolute authoritarianism throughout the child's life that is necessary during infancy and the first few ages in the life cycle. But neither does the parent attempt to become a peer with a child or try to live out personal unfulfilled ambitions through the child.

The best thing you can do for your children is to love your spouse. Never try to make a child into a substitute spouse. Keep your spouse the number one person in your life!

I have not discussed all the developmental tasks for young adults. I will leave the reader to illustrate them. The Church certainly has much help to offer with taking a civic responsibility and finding a congenial social group. "The thirties always present the maximum role demands" (Sheehy, 1995, p. 42).

I want to conclude this chapter by summarizing some statistics that Sheehy lists in *Passages* (1974, pp. 377-387) as "the crossroads for women." I hope you don't think I am giving undue attention to women. But the fact is that more women attend church than men and that more women seek out professional helpers with their problems than will men. Women in our time are in a peculiar circumstance of finding some new freedom that they are quite pleased with, but they still don't always know how to use it.

Thirty-five is the average age of mothers when they send their last child off to grade school. Thirty-five also begins the dangerous age for infidelity among women. Kinsey's figures showed that a wife is most likely to be unfaithful to her husband, if she ever is, in her late thirties when she is thinking, "This may be my last time to have a fling before I lose my looks." Thirty-five is the most common age of the runaway wife.

Thirty-five is literally the midpoint of life if we use the biblical life span of three score and ten. Thirty-five is when the average American woman reenters the working world. She may go to work for another twenty-four years.

Thirty-four is the average age at which the divorced woman will take a new husband. By this time, an average of thirteen years have elapsed since her first wedding day, and about six years since her divorce.

Thirty-five brings the biological boundary of motherhood rather clearly into sight. She can see the end of her ability to bear children fast approaching. More than that, women are pretty knowledgeable these days about the fact that the risk of giving birth to a child with Down's syndrome greatly increases as they get older. At twenty, the risk is about 1 in 2,000. But by thirty-five, it is about 1 in 1,000. By forty the risk is 1 in 100. In fact, some recent studies say that at age forty the risk may actually be 1 in 40.

By thirty-five, women who have not yet achieved motherhood are beginning to fear that they never will. The greatest number of adoptions by single women are made by women between the ages of thirty-five to thirty-nine. And married women frequently strive to have, as the case may be, their first, only, or last baby before age forty. These figures show that women at the age of thirty-five do seem to stand at the crossroads of life and may well be dealing with a lot of fear, frustration, and stress.

From one male viewpoint, Lord Byron titled the following poem, "On This Day I Complete My Thirty-Sixth Year":

> My days are in the yellow leaf;
>   The flowers and fruit of love are gone;
> The worm, the canker, and the grief
>   are mine alone.

We will see in the next four chapters what is happening developmentally to the children who are brought into the family.

Chapter 2

The Age of Grace:
Conception to Eighteen Months

I like to call the first period of life the "age of grace." Sigmund Freud and his followers call it the "oral phase." Erik Erikson calls it the period of "trust versus mistrust. Kegan (1982) characterizes selfhood in this stage as that of the incorporative self. I like to give these titles a theological twist, so it makes more sense to me to think of the time from birth to approximately a year and a half as the age of grace. (All of the ages in the life cycle are arbitrary and vary from one individual to another.)

We need to think first of all about prenatal development because some important things occur in the developing fetus before birth. Much is unknown, but one thing is certain. All of the nutritional needs of the fetus are met perfectly in the uterus. These needs will be met, even at the expense of the mother's body. Some years ago, before vitamins were regularly prescribed as a part of obstetrical care (and even today among women who omit such care or cannot afford vitamins), it was not unusual to see women who had given birth to two or three children wearing false teeth or whose teeth were largely decayed because their bodies had robbed the calcium from their teeth to give it to the baby for development of bones. So, if the mother's body must suffer, so be it; that seems to be the way of creation.

There's a nice word for this relationship between mother and child: "symbiosis." It is defined as the living together in intimate association, or even close union, of two organisms. This concept includes the mother perfectly meeting the biological and affectional needs of the child before birth. She feeds and protects it, but her own life is also enhanced by it. With quickening, parents begin to perceive the fetus as a separate individual and enter an intense relationship with the imagined child to be. And symbiosis jumps the hurdle of birth and continues to be appropriate even after birth as the mother tries to meet the biological and affectional needs of the child as much as possible.

Sons and Lovers by D. H. Lawrence (1982) is a novel concerning the symbiotic relationship between a mother and her son, probably D. H. Lawrence and his own mother. Paul, the main character, is a young man who tries to break away from his mother to commit himself in a love relationship with a woman his age. He never quite manages to do that, "to leave his mother," according to the biblical prescription in Genesis 2:24 and Matthew 19:5, "and be joined to his wife." The marriage never occurs. (Lawrence himself finally bonded with a woman about his mother's age and lived with her in Germany for several years.)

Birth itself is a separation experience. Otto Rank (1994), a disciple of Freud, made a big issue of this in saying that anxiety originates from the separation that occurs at birth, and throughout the rest of life much anxiety comes from the fear of separation. Rank said that birth was a crisis experience of pain as the infant leaves a comfortable, tested, and tried existence to experience a new kind of life. He thought psychologists had neglected the importance of the birth trauma. We almost smother in the (average) twenty-minute passage through the birth canal and gasp our way into the world of relationships. He found language replete with phrases that made references to it, such as feeling as though you have been "dragged through a keyhole," and other phrases that refer to the passage through the birth canal. We do not really know what the infant feels or how well developed the neurological system is, but we can be pretty sure that it is a tough day for the baby as well as the mother. There may well be some pain. The entrance into this world occurs in a rather cold (compared to the womb) room with bright lights shining immediately in the baby's eyes and a spank on the butt. It is not a very comfortable, welcoming sort of experience for the infant. Frederick LeBoyer, a French obstetrician, proposed in his book *Birth Without Violence* (1975) that things ought to be changed. He proposed that babies be delivered into a quieter, warmer, darker atmosphere. A small percentage of physicians have tried his suggestions experimentally. Very few have incorporated this method into their regular practice because the doctor cannot see very well. The frequent presence of the father in the delivery room in recent years does at least provide a person who has time to hold the baby instead of laying the infant on a cold, hard surface such as a scale.

FOOD AND LOVE

Right after birth, food and love become very important to an infant. The infant seems to have the right to expect or even demand food and care. This begins the one to one-and-a-half years in the baby's life when these needs are taken very seriously by parents or caregivers. People seriously try to meet all of the infant's needs that they possibly can. And they don't really ask anything in return, at least not at first. When you think about it, babies don't really have much to recommend them. They cry and demand care. They belch and pass gas. They puke and spit up. They are incontinent of bowel and bladder. They keep us awake and cost enormous sums of money. Yet we love them. Thus, I call this first period of life the age of grace. During this period, the parents do begin to convey some expectation for a return on their investment. But at first these parents do not seem to expect anything back from the baby at all. And for the infant, food and love get mixed together. To be loved is to be fed; to be fed is to be loved. So the child seems to develop a belief or assumption that "if you love me, you'll feed me; and if you feed me, you must love me." The child becomes addicted to the care, not just the mechanism that feeds. Food and love are rolled together in the baby's experience so that the child cannot distinguish one from the other.

The American Academy of Pediatrics recommends that all babies be breast-fed. The La Leche League is rather evangelistic about this. Breast-feeding does have advantages such as supplying the ideal nutrition during the early months as well as protection against infection and allergies. It also offers physical and psychological warmth that helps to promote the relationship between mother and infant.

During this time the child's primary relationships are with the father and especially the mother. All normal human beings are born with the capacity to form relationships. The concept of attachment (Wesley and Sullivan, 1986) that has come into the recent literature helps us to understand the beginning stages of forming relationships. Bonding is the term used to describe the parent's positive feelings toward the infant. The baby develops responsive smiling by six to eight months of age (Levine, Carey, and Crocker, 1992, p. 82). You have doubtlessly noticed how a mother and her infant can spend long periods of time with their faces very close together, looking intently into each other's eyes. That obviously satisfies both mother and child. This close touching (we are born with a gripping reflex) and gazing is very reassuring and comforting for both of them, and they devote long periods of time to doing just this. The mother's face and eyes become primary recognizable objects to the infant. She is usually the most permanent person in the baby's world. At a very early age, the baby learns to recognize these eyes, and this face, and this voice; partly because the infant has already heard that voice prenatally for months and months.

All of us have learned, probably by accident, that we get a better response from a baby if we talk in a high voice, similar to mother's voice. Men do it too. We have learned that an infant responds better, more quickly, and more intently to us if we raise the pitch of our voice. This is one way that men get in on the secondary bonding with babies in those early months.

In the age of grace, the infant experiences a little theology concerning omniscience, omnipotence, and omnipresence. It may seem to the baby that Mom is omniscient because she seems to know what needs to be done to provide comfort even when the infant is not sure. The infant knows of a sensation of hurting or discomfort but Mom often can figure that out even beyond the infant's ability to do so. And Mom certainly seems omnipotent, or all-powerful, and Dad even more so. Either can pick up the infant easily. Dad may even be a little more reckless than Mom and throw the baby into the air. In fact, the kid may get two messages out of that: one, this is fun, whee; but what if. . . . The infant learns a little about omnipresence but finds that this is the parent's first limitation. Parents really are not omnipresent though they seem to be at first. But there are times when the infant experiences that the parent is not present even though the baby rages and cries.

Freud is the one who pointed out that during this period the mouth is the erogenous zone. We are born with a sucking reflex. Thus Freud called it the oral phase of development. The mouth is the infant's contact with the world and everything experienced has to pass the "taste test." This is the way that the infant does reality testing to experience the world and begin to make distinctions between objects. So primary interests are centered in the mouth, with the intake of air, water, and food, along with making all kinds of sounds with the tongue and the voice. This all becomes very interesting and the infant will devote a lot of time to these kinds of activities.

During the time in mother's arms and/or at the breast, the infant seems to be in its most comfortable state. That is the infant's closest proximity to the prenatal stage. Some people think of the perfect time in life as being prenatal, or in very early childhood. The traditional Christian view of heaven as a place where all our needs will be perfectly met borders on this early state of existence: being held in Mom's arms with all of our needs supplied. Some psychologists refer to this as the primal scene. Babies sometimes learn certain mannerisms that are reminiscent of this primal experience. One of our sons developed a sucking motion, and often when he was a little frustrated, we could see him doing that little sucking motion with his mouth as a way of comforting himself. Self-consoling behavior marks the beginning of autonomy. Of course a more obvious and common habit is thumb sucking. About half of all infants do that as a way of comforting themselves and trying to take themselves to that place where they would really like to be at the moment. Sleeping in a nice bed under warm blankets is a nightly attempt to return to the womb, symbolically at least. I have learned to love a water bed because it is even more cuddling than a cold, hard mattress. It is warm when I get in it, and fits itself around my body so that in bed with the covers around me I make my nightly attempt to return to this heavenly place where I experience early life and get ready for the next day.

PAIN AND RAGE

In addition to food and love, babies experience pain and rage. After birth, the child experiences for the first time hunger, loud noises, dryness, hardness, and greater extremes of hot and cold. In the prenatal stage some of these things have been experienced, but in muffled, modified kinds of ways. After birth these kinds of experiences are greatly accentuated. The word "homeostasis" means the tendency of an organism to maintain within itself relatively stable conditions. Our bodies do that biologically and we try to do that emotionally with our minds. The body tries to maintain stable temperature and chemical composition and so forth by means of its own regulatory mechanisms such as sweating and pulse rate, heartbeat, breath frequency, and so forth. Homeostasis is upset, for example, when hunger occurs. At first the stomach feels more of the discomfort, but after just a little while the stomach begins to share that sensation of pain with the whole body, until finally it seems that every cell of the body is bearing its little bit of this feeling of hunger. Birth also interrupts the infant's homeostasis. And after birth it is never as perfect again. When homeostasis is interrupted, anger is felt. Then the infant begins to call out to express this inner feeling of anger. Crying is a kind of call: "If there is someone out there who hears me, come and help me." If the crying does not quickly produce a helping person, then the infant begins to rage.

If raging doesn't produce the desired results, then the child begins to try some other methods of communicating need, such as whimpering, or begging for pity. Emotional beggars may be born even in these early days. "Canalization" is a word that Gardner Murphy (1949), a psychologist, coined for people who are set in their ways emotionally. Sometimes an infant, having learned that parents do not seem to respond to crying or raging but will respond to begging or whimpering or sounding pitiful, will learn to give out that kind of communication when they experience needs. As infants we begin to learn to love and move with people, to hate and move against people, or to withdraw and move away from people.

Rage sometimes brings rejection. In other words, the parent may handle the baby roughly if the infant has already begun raging before the parent appears. So the infant experiences this feeling of rejection from the parent and may therefore even learn to reject himself or herself. A baby's anger should not destroy a parent's affection or care, but parents are human and sometimes it does at least change the way the care is given.

Even at this stage, children begin to displace love from persons to things. That is one reason we give teddy bears and other soft inanimate objects to babies. Winnicott (1965) called such things "transitional objects." They can rage against these objects. They can bite them and beat them against the side of the crib or throw them out of the crib because these objects will never reject them. Once they are back within the grasp of the infant, they are still soft and cuddly. They don't bite back or reject. They can stand the rage and still be present and available.

COMMON PROBLEMS

One of the common problems that may occur during the age of grace is that the child does not eat much. Parents become very concerned about this and quickly hustle the child to the doctor. Pediatricians are said to "eat" because children will not eat. Vomiting, constipation, or diarrhea are three more common problems in infancy that arouse parental concern and are dealt with often by physicians. There is the medical diagnosis of failure to thrive. Some infants have a lot of problems with food. They don't eat well and they do not grow and gain weight normally. They can die. Failure to thrive seems to be connected to the amount of love and affection that the infant experiences or does not experience. It can be a serious problem in their physical health.

Separation anxiety is another common problem in the age of grace. Some children experience an inability to leave their parents without panic. Babies are learning to trust and become addicted to the object of care. So staying with a baby-sitter may be frightening to a child in the latter part of this stage. This phenomenon is called stranger anxiety. The child needs to be told repeatedly "Mommy and Daddy will be back." Attachment can become a problem if it's not completed well.

Holding the breath is another problem that concerns parents. Some infants start this even at this age; for some it comes later. It's a kind of temper tantrum and has a delightfully disturbing effect on parents. No need to worry though. We have never lost a child to death or even unconsciousness by breath-holding.

Autism probably occurs because of lack of bonding. These children don't respond to adults or other children. They seem to pull back into their inner world and they don't interact. They make no attempt to communicate. This may even develop into schizophrenia. It can be a very serious problem.

Colic and croup are very common problems and extremely worrisome for parents. They may sometimes be emotional in origin.

SIDS, sudden infant death syndrome, is a tragic problem. The child suddenly dies and the reason for death is very difficult to ascertain. Parents may think they have neglected their child and feel guilty. An infant death that was apparently SIDS is reported in the Bible in 1 Kings 3:19. The final diagnosis by many pathologists that is told to the parents is simply, sudden infant death syndrome.

Child abuse, strange as it seems to most minds, does occur. It appears to be handed down from one generation to the next as a learned behavior: persons who were abused as children tend to abuse their own children.

Developmental delay is the last problem I'll mention in this section. The child simply does not develop at the rate that children ordinarily do in comparison to well-established norms.

Pediatricians and psychologists commonly agree that we are created with only two fears: falling and loud noises. These are part of the package deal. All our other fears are learned. In this age period, after bonding occurs, we learn to fear separation from our parents. Fear of strangers may begin around the seventh month, but it may become more prominent in the next stage of growth.

REGRESSION TO THE AGE OF GRACE

Regression is an unconscious attempt to return to an earlier stage in life. All of us have some sort of need to get back beyond the time of our first frustration, to when life was really good—at least better than we currently know it. I want to discuss some adult attempts to move back to the age of grace.

It's not difficult to think of the car as a symbolic uterus. In an automobile we assume a fetal position. We bounce along as we drive or ride, protected from the bumps by the springs, shocks, and rubber tires. Sounds nearby are muffled by the car around us. Heat or cold are tempered because we're in a protected environment. Everything is muffled to protect us and we kind of float along, carried as Mother's body once carried us, absorbing some of the bumps. Some of us like to drive for pleasure. Many people go for a

Sunday afternoon drive because it's such a pleasant experience. It's an attempt at regression.

Eating and drinking bring oral gratification and may involve oral regression. Some adults in our society especially like to drink from bottles. Alcoholics, if you listen to them, love to talk about their "bottle." Chewing gum and smoking are probably an attempt to get back to this age of grace. Talking itself is an oral activity. Preachers and teachers have an orally oriented vocation. Clergy are considered to be oral personalities who like to eat, talk, and perhaps chew gum as well. And it's interesting to think about one of the important events in our churches as an oral religious experience, the ritual that we Christians call by various names: the Lord's Supper, Communion, Eucharist, Mass. The basic ground of fellowship among many religious groups is eating together. If you want to get a good crowd, or celebrate a significant event, you have a dinner of some kind, a meal. We incorporate into our worship, as Jesus taught us to do, the concept of eating.

Perhaps men's interest in female breasts is partly related to the time at Mother's breast. Maybe this isn't such an adult, macho thing as we men often like to think it is, but rather a kind of infantile interest that we developed a long time ago in quite another setting.

ORAL AGGRESSION

Babies are sometimes said to bite the nipple or to bite the hand that feeds them. Some animals protect themselves and harm others with their mouths. The mouth is their defensive and offensive weapon of protection or to get food and stay alive. We humans can be orally aggressive and we sometimes do so by spitting or biting, or by the words we use. Some phrases in our language are heard and used unconsciously to emphasize this. We talk about "chewing people out": "The boss chewed me out today." Or we talk about being unable to "swallow" something somebody else has said, or being unable to "stomach" some things. We talk about people eating themselves to death. We talk about digging a grave with a knife and fork. These are examples of oral aggression.

LIFE CYCLE TRAITS OF THE AGE OF GRACE

So, this first stage of life is, I think, characterized by grace. We come into a world where there are "giants" around us who try to meet our needs, and they don't ask anything of us at first. But as we move on into this first year and a half, we begin to experience some expectation on the part of these giants. They seem to respond positively to us when we behave in certain ways. When we make a particular little muscle movement on our faces, spreading our mouths in what becomes known as a social smile, we get a favorable response out of these adults around us. We get a message that they like that. So we learn to do that more. We spread our mouths just right, and these big people clap and cheer for us and seem to give us a lot of encouragement. That feels good, even powerful. So we give them a lot of that. It appears to satisfy them.

But then we begin to experience another expectation from them. They give us a lot of attention, while sitting us upright on our little bottoms. They hold us and talk to us and everything seems to be so wonderful until they suddenly let go. We rock back over and maybe bump our heads on the bed or something. At first we can't quite figure this out. What do the giants want now? One of our fears is the fear of falling. Somehow, we get a message from the giants that they expect something back from us now. And they keep working with us until we finally decide that to please these adults we're going to have to really bear down with our little muscles and make our bodies sit up. So we work hard and learn to do it even when they let go. We can sit there for a long time, and we begin to notice this wonderful response we're getting from these giants, so we begin to feel powerful again. Everything is wonderful . . .

Until they begin to stand us up on our feet. One day they've got us propped up in a corner, and they shake rattles in our faces to distract us. Then they let go of us and down we go. Or they get us out in the middle of the floor on a nice soft rug and they stand us up and make all kinds of noise to get us thinking about something else then let go again and we crumble. Again we're getting this message. The age of grace is not quite perfect. We have to learn to respond to the demands of the giants. After we learn to stand alone, the age of grace is wonderful for a short while.

Then they want us to start walking, then talking, and so on. So the age of grace is imperfect except for the first few weeks or months. But I think the term is nevertheless more characteristic than any other theological word for this time in life.

Neonate: Zero to Four Weeks

a. Gross motor—hands fisted
b. Language—throaty sounds
c. Fine motor—stares at surroundings
d. Personal-social—regards face
e. Cognitive—sensorimotor reflex—noncognitive
f. Normal fears—aloneness, sudden noise, loss of support, dark
g. Developmental task—eating, sleeping, eliminating, respiration
h. Defenses—incorporation, elimination
i. Normal autistic phase

Early Infancy: Three Months

a. Gross motor—head up. Supports weight on forearms
b. Language—coo, laugh, social, turns to voice
c. Fine motor—eyes follow past midline, grasps rattle, transfers cube
d. Personal-social—social, smiles
e. Cognitive—eye-hand coordination, primary circular reaction, imitation, beginning internalization of the object
f. Normal fears—loss of mother and father
g. Developmental task—capacity to postpone, attachment begins
h. Defenses—incorporation, elimination
i. Symbiotic phase—rudimentary ego—beginning attachment

Middle Infancy: Six Months

a. Gross motor—sits
b. Language—crows, babbles
c. Fine motor—hand to hand, release
d. Personal-social—stranger anxiety, shows likes and dislikes
e. Cognitive—sensorimotor, expresses needs instinctively

  f. Fears—loss of mother, strangers anxiety
  g. Developmental task—learning to function, attachment transitional
  h. Defenses—introjection, projection, denial
  i. Symbiotic phase—rudimentary superego

Late Infancy: Nine Months

  a. Gross motor—sits alone, stands briefly, creeps, prehensile release
  b. Language—imitates sounds, one word, heeds name," "dada" or "mama"
  c. Fine motor—combines two cubes
  d. Personal-social—pat-a-cake, peek-a-boo, feeds self crackers
  e. Cognitive—sensorimotor reflexes cognitively
  f. Fears—stranger anxiety
  g. Developmental task—learning trust
  h. Defenses—crying
  i. Separation-individuation phase, fully attached

End of Infancy: Twelve to Eighteen Months

  a. Gross motor—walks
  b. Language—two or three words
  c. Fine motor—release cube in cup
  d. Personal-social—dressing, solitary play, finger foods, drinks from cup, comes when called
  e. Cognitive—looks for hidden object
  f. Fears—stranger anxiety
  g. Developmental task—differentiate self from other, begin self-control
  h. Defenses—turning against self, negation
  i. Object relations—separation, individuation

Note: One of the best sources of information (which is updated periodically) for the development of infants through adolescents is on the Internet. It is Bright Futures at <www.brightfutures.org>.

Chapter 3

The Age of Works:
Eighteen Months to Three Years

The age of works lasts approximately from the ages of eighteen months to three years. During this time, children attain half of their adult height (Levine, Carey, and Crocker, 1992, p. 97). Kegan (1982) names the style of selfhood at this stage the impulsive self. Fowler (1987, p. 59) said that from about the time children begin to use language to communicate, he sees the emergence of a style of meaning making he calls the "intuitive-projective stage." These children live in a world of magic where cartoon characters seem real, and they may have an imaginary friend.

TIMELINESS

Time and order begin to be imposed by the parents on the life of the child. This usually begins in the second year. Time imposes itself on our lives; we learn to live by it. We find some way to measure time. We usually think of time being measured by the sun, because daylight and darkness equal a day. We measure our days into weeks, weeks into months, and months into years.

But when we stop to think about it, time has been measured in other ways. In fact, there is evidence that in some biblical periods time may have been measured by the moon. The measurement of time in 365 ¼ days per year according to the sun is certainly not, as a measurement, as old as the Hebrew scriptures. Many primitive people measured their time by the moon. That is another way to measure time.

Women tend to measure time by the month according to their menstrual cycles. They have a built-in clock that men don't really know much about.

Time can be measured in other ways. All of us have a built-in biological way of measuring time, which has to do with our hunger or appetite. Even on a cloudy day when we do not wear a watch, we still have some idea of when to eat. My two youngest sons and I did a seventeen-mile hike in Missouri on the Big Piney Trail. We set out early one morning without a watch. We walked and walked over hills and valleys until we were really hungry. We knew it must be lunchtime. The sun was high in the sky, and we made a Boy Scout clock by driving a stick upright in the ground and drawing a circle around it. We were hungry, so we ate lunch. Then during a long afternoon of hiking, we decided it couldn't have been later than about 10:30 a.m. when we had lunch. So the stomach isn't a very accurate time measurement.

Another way to measure the time is by breathing. This rhythmical biological apparatus helps us measure time. Doctors and nurses count how many breaths we take in a minute, and we must have some sense of that too. For instance, when a baby is crying, maybe it has some notion of how long it has been crying by how many breaths it has taken.

The first measurement of time that any baby ever knows about is the sound of the regular beating of the mother's heart even before the baby is born. The fetus can easily hear its mother's heartbeat and that becomes a stabilizing rhythmic sound that the fetus relies on. Hearing that beat is a part of existence before birth. If you want to soothe an infant, music won't do it, but rhythm will. After eighteen months of research, Dr. Lee Salk (brother of Dr. Jonas Salk), along with some engineers, perfected the Securitone—a reproduction of the mother's heartbeat (Salk reported the conclusions of his study at the meeting of the World Federation of Mental Health on August 10, 1960, in Edinburgh, Scotland). Today you can buy recordings for infants that have a little music on top for the parents so they will think they're getting their money's worth—but underneath the music is the simulated rhythm of what mother's heartbeat sounded like to the fetus in the prenatal state. Infants seem to be comforted by these recordings, so the infant knows something about time.

The idea of time, of course, is quite old. Calendars have existed since ancient times. Time, as a concept, is a masculine idea. We talk about father time and about grandfather clocks. As a masculine idea, time is rigid, unbending, and it is the same for everybody. It cannot be changed. We can rebel against time by procrastinating, but we don't get away with it. We don't really make any more time for ourselves by doing that. As people become more civilized, they seem to become more time conscious. They order their lives with time. There is a time to do this and a time to do that, even as pointed out in the Bible in Ecclesiastes 3:1-8:

> For everything there is a season, and a time for every matter under heaven: a time to be born, and a time to die; a time to plant, and a time to pluck up what is planted;
>
> a time to kill, and a time to heal; a time to break down, and a time to build up;
>
> a time to weep, and a time to laugh; a time to mourn, and a time to dance;
>
> a time to cast away stones, and a time to gather stones together; a time to embrace, and a time to refrain from embracing;
>
> a time to seek, and a time to lose; a time to keep, and a time to cast away;
>
> a time to rend, and a time to sew; a time to keep silence, and a time to speak;
>
> a time to love, and a time to hate; a time for war, and a time for peace.

Primitive people were not as time conscious as we are. If you've read Jonathan Swift's story, *Gulliver's Travels* (1726), you'll remember that the Lilliputians found Gulliver asleep and tied him up until they made friends with him. They thought that he carried his god in his pocket because frequently through the day (after they untied him), he would stop, pause and pull a circular instrument out of his pocket, bow over it, and meditate. It was his pocket watch, but they thought it was his God. Americans have been characterized by cartoonists as a guy standing on a street corner under a huge clock looking at his wristwatch. We are time conscious in so many ways.

Procrastination is a kind of childish rebellion against time. We're limited by time, God made us that way. Yet God himself does not seem to be limited by time. Thus, he's not as time conscious as we are. We pray and say, "God, do it now!" We get very disappointed and upset sometimes if He doesn't respond. We sometimes talk about God's own good time *(kairos)*. But if I want something, I want it in my time *(chronos)*. We try to impose our time on God.

Society has tried to set the minister apart to listen to the sound of a different drummer and to keep time by other kinds of rules and regulations than most people do. But clergy become extremely time conscious and frequently get into the ritual of the black book, during which the pocket calendar is meditated over and carefully marked. Unfortunately, I am tied to mine far more than I thought I would permit myself to be. Even though society tries by ordination to set clergy aside to allow us to use time differently, we usually get right into time competition with others. We tell people so often in our sermons how busy we are that they get a little "gun shy" of us. They need our help, but first they'll say, "Pastor, I know you're busy, but could you possibly . . ." That's a sad commentary on the way clergy present themselves to their people.

ORDERLINESS

When a child is about one and one-half years old, parents begin to introduce some new demands. These have to do not only with time, but also with order. By now, the child is sitting, crawling, walking, running, climbing, talking, doing all kinds of things, and getting into all kinds of things. The child now moves into the age of works and begins to learn something about orderliness. Parents communicate to the child that orderliness is important. There is a certain place for everything. Everything ought to be in its place. There's a certain way to do this and a certain way to do that. There's a place where things ought to be kept. "Your food is supposed to be on your plate or in your mouth, and you're not supposed to put it on your stomach. Your belly button won't suck it in, and it doesn't go in your hair." So they begin to teach the child about order. Timeliness and orderliness are taught in many ways.

CLEANLINESS

Another focus during this stage of life is on cleanliness. The child begins to get the message that "Mommy and Daddy love a clean baby" and that "cleanliness is next to godliness." Some kids misinterpret that message quite early and never quite get over it. They think that cleanliness *is* godliness. Some people really stay confused about that. They become fastidious about cleanliness. Some mothers have a real problem with their children at this age. They want to keep them as clean as possible, and they won't permit them to get dirty. The child's freedom is thus restricted in terms of exploring the world. Natural curiosity is inhibited.

The major focus at this period of life, according to Freud and many others, is on toilet training. Freud called this the "anal phase" because the anus was the bodily opening that came into prominence in this time of life: the oral cavity during the age of grace and now the anal orifice during the age of works. Toilet training becomes the focus of what goes on between the mother, father, and child. Toilet training takes place early in this period in many families. Some parents are perhaps a little too eager and expect too much too soon of their children. Some boast that they have their child toilet trained by the time the child is one year old. I always wonder if maybe the mother hasn't trained herself rather than the child: she has learned when to sit the child on the potty. Neurologically, children don't usually gain control of the sphincter muscles that open and close the anus until they get beyond one year of age. Many are closer to two years old before they have gained sufficient neurological control of that muscle to actually begin to manipulate it at will. If the child is given time to understand what is expected and the ability physiologically to perform that feat, then toilet training can be accomplished rather quickly. Two researchers have demonstrated how toilet training can be accomplished in one day (Azrin and Foxx, 1974). However, many parents place their child in competition with those of their friends and don't have the patience to wait for their child to reach the appropriate age for toilet training. Toilet training encompasses timeliness, orderliness, and cleanliness.

Digestion is another measurement of time; the measurement of how long it takes food to pass from the mouth to the anus. When the urge to defecate comes it is only a matter of time before you've got to satisfy the need to excrete the waste. Parents begin to teach the child orderliness. "Look, this substance should not be in your diaper; it's supposed to be over there in the potty." There is order to this; certain places for certain things. "No, your food and your toys do not belong in the potty!" Cleanliness is taught well.

Some unfortunate things occur because many parents teach their kids that they are dirty. We start by teaching them to abhor the odor of feces. None of us comes equipped to automatically dislike the smell of feces; we learn this. We also have to learn that perfume and food smell good. So, children learn to dislike a part of themselves. Something that they have produced in their bodies and excreted into the world smells bad and is dirty. You put it only in this one certain place, noplace else. Then Mommy wrinkles her nose and quickly flushes it away. So children may come to abhor their bodily products, what they can create and produce for the world.

Children also get into a real bargaining position. For the first time in life, they say "No." Mother says, "Do it right here and now." The child can say, "No." And there is little Mom can say or do to force the child at this point. Some mothers get too aggressive and get out the enema equipment. But you know, that's not fair. That is rape. That is robbery.

The first moral sense comes into being during the age of works. This is a part of the conscience. The message from the parents and society is "You've got to be good." But the first moral sense is negative. It's "no." You can't find a child in this age group that doesn't say no, a number of times a day. It is a normal part of human growth and development. They discover that they can arbitrate. No matter how many times mother may sit them on the potty and beg and plead, all they have to say is "No." On the other hand, no matter how much mothers may say, "Now don't fill your pants," they can do it, and there's nothing she can do about it.

Children begin to get a feeling of control over their bodies. They also find out if they put the right stuff in the right place at the right time that Mother and Dad will brag about them. They seem to think as follows: "This stuff that I produce must have some value. Maybe it's more valuable than I had thought. Mom and Dad make such a fuss over it if I put it in the right place. And if I put it in the wrong place, they act like it really bothers them." A lot of kids thus decide that they have something that they can give the world, something that the world wants.

Some get the idea that if they put on an advertising campaign, business will boom. So they begin to advertise a little bit by spreading feces around on the walls and urine on the floor here and there thinking that these samples will make their product more desirable. They soon learn that unless the stuff is put in the right place that it's not wanted at all. It's considered dirty.

The anus is closely related to the first moral sense. To get along in this world, you have to learn something about cleanliness, timeliness, and orderliness. If you procrastinate and don't deal with time, you're not going to stop playing soon enough to get to the potty chair and get your pants down and put your stuff in the right place in an orderly manner. If you let that stuff get in your pants, it makes you dirty and only Mom can clean you up again. The first moral sense is largely contingent on what children do with the anal opening. They begin to learn some further distinctions between what is good and what is bad or what is praised and what is condemned. It is very important to learn these during the age of works because they can never be learned as well later.

Frustration and anger develop in children as they try to meet the demands of parents and sometimes are unable to do that. The more you can give them praise and reward for doing the right thing the better. Punishment can certainly be overdone. Lots of little kids are spanked during early toilet training when physiologically they cannot control the anus. They are punished as though they are doing it on purpose to get even with Mom or Dad. I think praise is the best way of teaching anything whether the person is two or eighty-two years old. Punishment may help a little but praise works better. I hope you see why I call it the age of works. The child has to work to get parental praise. It doesn't come freely as it did in the first year or so of life.

COMMON PROBLEMS

Several common problems occur during the age of works. One of the problems that emerges during this time is called "night terrors."

These are scary dreams or nightmares. The child is very frightened and may awaken at night screaming and crying.

We were probably the most strict with our oldest child in the toilet training phase. That is very typical of parents. We were learning to be parents and very insecure. We were not sure we could get our son toilet trained. We had never tried to do it before. The oldest child teaches the parents a lot. Younger brothers and sisters profit a great deal by the oldest child's hard knocks. Our oldest child would wake up at night terrified. He could hardly awaken even though his eyes would be open. He might be moving, walking, drinking water, talking. He was really frightened by these night terrors, and we were too.

What happens is that the child's conscience is beginning to develop, and in dreams, the child does things that are against the first moral sense. Something in the dreams chases, frightens, or threatens the child. These are often large animals such as bears, and all kinds of things. If you want an interpretation of those dreams, the animals are probably disguised parents who have now started punishing the child in regard to toilet training and other things. The child can tell parents about being scared by a bear who chased him in his dream. He doesn't have to say, "Dad, you were chasing me with a belt in my dream." Mothers frequently take their children to physicians to find out what causes night terrors. Night terrors will persist well beyond the time of toilet training, but this is when they are most severe. The child may become very fearful of the punishing parent who is not very patient and who expects a lot of compliance very soon. Children may project their fear on many things, but basically their major fear is displeasing their parents.

Constipation and diarrhea are also problems. Over-the-counter remedies or a trip to the doctor usually takes care of them. Holding the breath is another problem. The child learns that "I can really scare Mom if I hold my breath." It's very hard to hold your breath at will long enough to pass out. If Mom stops reacting to it, the problem almost always fades away.

Tantrums become a typical emotional expression for some children when they feel thwarted or frustrated by the world. Fascination with monsters and superheroes is a way in which play is used to master typical feelings of vulnerability.

Speech problems such as stuttering commonly begin at this time, though they can begin later. Very often, they are connected with fear. The child is trying so hard to please the parent, he or she is almost afraid to say anything. Also, shyness may be connected to problems that develop in this age period.

There is a phenomenon called anal regression: attempts to return to the anal stage of life. Freud talked about an "anal character." Three words summarize it. One is "perfectionist." Anal characters are perfectionists. They try to keep perfectly to the rules of cleanliness, orderliness, and timeliness. The second word is "pedantic" or "precisionistic." They may go into a kind of job or field that calls for great precision, absolutely having every last thing right. The last word is "petulant"; they are angry, threatening, and easily offended. Some other words descriptive of the anal character are clean, orderly, aggressive, miserly, and anxiety ridden. Anal characters carry part of this phase with them throughout life.

Economy is sometimes emotionally related to this period of time in life. For instance, money is called filthy lucre and is often treated much like feces. Parents are in horror if they see their child with money in his or her mouth. You can hardly conceive of a dirty bank or a dirty, unkempt person working there. The church treasurer is usually a rather fastidious person.

Many people have a certain amount of obsessive compulsiveness. These traits have their beginnings in the age of works. An obsession is a recurrent thought that comes back again and again in your mind. This happens to all of us at some time with some tune we have heard on the radio or at church. You find yourself humming it, whistling it. You finally get tired of it, and you still do it anyway.

A compulsion is a repetitive act, something that is done over and over again even though you don't especially want to do it or like to do it. All of us want to be somewhat compulsive. We want to give some attention to repetition. If we don't, we may not be able to hold a job. We have to be somewhat obsessive and compulsive to study hard enough to complete an education. I certainly would not have my degrees if I were not compulsive.

Psychologists think they can trace the beginning vocational interest of painters or artists to the anal phase of life—smearing smelly paint with a brush is an acceptable way to make a living. Collectors are perfectionistic. Stamp and coin collecting are fairly common hobbies. It is a matter of wanting everything in its place. The age of works is where that motivation and that inner urge develops.

There is also anal aggression. Adolescents and sometimes even adults write on the walls of public privies, in the rest rooms of court houses, bus stations, and filling stations. That certainly is anal aggression. We can be grateful they are not writing with the substance they unconsciously would like to use on the walls.

Sociopathy has its beginning during the age of works if parents do not take toilet training seriously and enforce the rules of timeliness, orderliness, and cleanliness. Sociopaths or psychopaths are persons who have not developed the ability to judge the difference between right and wrong. They have not learned to internalize Mother and Dad's (or society's) sense of values. Later on they may learn that if they get caught doing something wrong, they will be punished. They become liars, thieves, or bad check writers and worse because they cannot distinguish between what is right and what is wrong.

Children learn to identify during this time in life with the parent of the same gender. A little girl can be taught to sit on the potty chair, and she doesn't have problems with that. But there comes a time in the little boy's training when he rebels and says, "No, Mom, I want to stand up like Dad." Unless children at this age can begin to make some primary identification with the parent of the same sex, their toilet training is going to take much longer. But if parents are gracious enough to give a boy the privilege of standing up and facing that potty chair and doing the best he can at hitting it, then he is doing it like Dad, and he feels better about that.

Is there any theology in these events that happen so early in life? How does this pertain to the Church? In the Hebrew Bible, we have the law: the Ten Commandments and many other laws. Many people see that as the place where the Church is or at least ought to be: with the law. In the Christian Scriptures, the Pharisees had much to say about keeping the law. Jesus chided the Pharisees because they were such anal characters (though he obviously didn't use that term). They had added many new laws to those in the Old Testament and were very legalistic about keeping the law. They complained to Jesus because his disciples didn't go through all the rituals of washing their hands before and after a meal as good Jews did. Some people say this is what the Church ought to be doing today: strongly enforcing the law:, "Thou shalt not! Thou shalt."

Then we have this whole business of evil as well. All kinds of things go on in the realm of evil: human wickedness and natural calamities. Greeks, barbarians, and philosophers were described in the Bible as being evil in the way they thought, behaved, and taught. People in the time of Jesus and Paul were confronted with the mystery religions which were sexually oriented, using temple prostitutes.

Psychologically, we can talk about Eden, which represents the id, and the law, which represents the superego. Jesus and the new covenant, the good news, and the new birth are somewhere between Eden and the law representing the ego. In my opinion, human beings are created with the freedom of choice, and we sometimes choose to do something we know is wrong. We may have a natural capacity to lie or steal, but we can learn much about how to refine these activities from society. Thus, we accumulate evil within us. The id is packaged with the infant at birth. The superego begins to develop by the end of the first year. The ego is the last of these three entities to develop. It is the battleground for the conflicts between the id and superego and is where decisions are made. I think the teachings of Jesus and the work of the Holy Spirit influence us mostly at the level of the ego. The law influences us at the level of the superego.

Some ministers think that the Church's main task is to strengthen the superego or the conscience. The best compliment anyone could ever give these ministers is to call them "the conscience of the community." Maybe that is all right, but I have questions about it. Pinocchio was a sociopath (Gaylin, 1990). He didn't really know the difference between good and evil. When he lied, his nose grew longer. He had a friend who played the part of his conscience: that was Jiminy Cricket, who sat on his shoulder and told him the difference between right and wrong. I'm not sure that it is the Church's job or the pastor's job to sit on people's shoulders and play Jiminy Cricket, telling them the difference between good and evil: Thou shalt and thou shalt not. I think our task, rather, is to help people find the freedom that Christ talked about that frees us both from the literal, heavy, hard, unbending law and the terrible, bad evil with its consequences. I think that the Lord wants to help us find the freedom to be ourselves in light of the law and in fear of evil.

If parents are consistent in toilet training, the child is going to do reasonably well as long as parents praise the desired behavior and are patient. The child gets messed up most of all when parents are inconsistent. One time they praise lavishly, but next time they don't praise at all. Sometimes they punish harshly and the child doesn't know quite what to expect for his or her behavior.

No two brothers or sisters are alike even though the same parents toilet trained both children. No two children are toilet trained the same way because parents grow older and wiser and more experienced.

Ezekiel chided the Israelites for believing the proverb that "the fathers have eaten sour grapes, and the children's teeth are set on edge" (Ezek. 18:2). Ezekiel clarified that "the soul that sins shall die" (Ezek. 18:4). The soul that sins will be responsible for the sin. Jeremiah said that God's new covenant would be between God and the individual rather than between God and the nation. Even then, people were being seen theologically by the Hebrews as being responsible for the self only. Jesus came along and, with his two-edged sword, cut the generations apart. He had a lot to say about who is our mother, who are our brothers, who are our sisters. So the New Testament emphasizes individuality even more. The child is an individual created by God, and each child will react differently.

LIFE CYCLE TRAITS OF THE AGE OF WORKS

Infancy: Eighteen Months

    a. Gross motor—kicks, throws, walks
    b. Language—naming, uses six or seven words
    c. Fine motor—tower of four cubes, scribbles
    d. Personal-social—toilet, begins to imitate housework, etc., parallel play
    e. Cognitive—applying familiar meaning to new situations
    f. Fears—loss of love, separation anxiety

g. Developmental tasks—feeds from spoon
h. Defenses—uses "no"
i. Mastery of space with large muscles

Preschool: Two Years Old

a. Gross motor—balances on one foot
b. Language—phrases—uses two- or three-word sentences
c. Fine motor—tower of six cubes, imitate circular motion and V motion
d. Personal-social—plays with others
e. Cognitive—preconceptual phase, egocentric perspective, outward appearances
f. Fears—auditory, separation
g. Developmental task—character, beginning conscience formation, toilet training
h. Defenses—act of negation, turning against self
i. Walking mastery

Preschool: Three Years Old

a. Gross motor—tricycle, stairs
b. Language—sentences, answers simple question
c. Fine motor—draw circle, imitate a cross
d. Personal-social—separates easily from mother, knows sex, cooperative and group play
e. Cognitive—egocentric, imagination, animism
f. Fears—visual, loss of love or approval
g. Developmental task—learning to function, attachment transitional
h. Defenses—imitation, repression
i. Separation-individuation complete, declaration of independence, sense of time

Chapter 4

The Age of Family Romance:
Three to Six Years

The stage of development that in psychoanalysis is called the "oedipal period," Erikson characterizes as "autonomy versus shame and doubt." I like to call it the "age of family romance." It is at this early age in life that children first begin to discover the "forbidden fruit." Children are not very knowledgeable, and they are naturally curious. So they explore the world and discover all kinds of things.

FORBIDDEN FRUIT

By the time they get to be three to six years of age, children begin to discover unexplored areas of themselves, including their genital organs. They touch and handle these and find it pleasurable. Also, they get interested in figuring out what is different about boys and girls. They soon decide that it must be more than their hairstyles. It is a natural curiosity often expressed by playing "doctor" or "house."

They are exploring themselves just as they explore the rest of the world. But they discover this "forbidden fruit" because they notice that touching their genital organs really disturbs these giants that they live with called parents. They discover, "Gosh, when I touch this even these giants tremble. They can hardly stand it." Parents or caregivers begin to convey a message to children in one way or another that "there is a tree in the midst of the garden; do not touch it lest you die." This begins to bring a great deal of attention to the genital organs because children find them pleasurable to touch. A lot of feelings surround these organs. The genital organ seems to become omnipotent. "It seems to be really powerful, the most powerful thing about me," the child may begin to think. The genitals come to be the most prominent erogenous or pleasurable zone.

Another phrase that you see in the literature is "genital phase." The prominence has passed from the oral cavity to the anus and now from the anus to the genital organs. This is the newly discovered pleasurable organ that begins to get a lot of attention. The fact that it is forbidden, mysterious, pleasurable, and powerful makes it even more enticing.

The child moves into the age of family romance, and identification with the parent of the same gender takes on new developments. Identification certainly began at least as early as the age of works, but it progresses and develops in this stage because children begin to identify even more closely and clearly, usually with the parent of the same gender. They begin to realize that "my genitals are like Dad's or Sister is like Mother," and so the identification progresses.

An interesting thing about human beings is that we seem to labor with the notion that we could become either sex, that it is not really predetermined or biological. So a boy identifies with his father primarily and his mother secondarily and vice versa for a girl.

As a part of his identification with his dad, a boy notices that Dad loves this person of the opposite sex: Mom. The boy then wants a woman like Dad's. "I want a girl just like the girl that married dear old Dad." He is male and the nearest, handiest female is Mom. The little boy begins to love his mother, similar to the way he understands his dad to love his mother. This is the beginning of the Oedipus complex.

THE OEDIPUS MYTH

The Greek myth of Oedipus on which Freud based his theory is as follows. There was a king in a certain country whose name was Laeus. He was the king of Thebes, and he didn't want his wife Jocasta to have a child because the oracle had said that if he had a child, his child would murder him and take his place. The king believed in these oracles. So he tried not to have a child. But on one occasion, he got drunk and slept with his wife. She conceived and bore a son. Since the oracle had said that his son would kill him, he drove a nail through his newborn son's feet and carried him off to a mountain where he left him to die. This was commonly done to unwanted children in ancient Greece.

The child was found by neighboring Corinthians and was named Oedipus, which means "swollen foot" in Greek. He was adopted by the Corinthian king and queen, who were childless. Oedipus grew to manhood. He loved the king and queen and thought they were his natural parents. One day on a visit to the Delphic oracle, he asked what his future would be. The oracle said that he was going to kill his father and marry his mother. He left in great horror because he loved his parents. In fact, he was so upset at the thought that he never returned to Corinth.

In his wandering, he was walking one day on a narrow road. A carriage came along and ran over his foot. In a burst of anger, he stopped the carriage and flung the passenger to the road. In the process the passenger's foot was caught in the reigns, and he was killed by the horses. The passenger was none other than Laeus, King of Thebes. Oedipus didn't know that and journeyed on toward Thebes.

Just outside of Thebes, there was a great Sphinx, a monster perched on the mount who terrorized the people. If people tried to leave or enter Thebes, the Sphinx asked them to solve his riddle: "What walks on four legs in the morning, two legs in the afternoon, and three legs in the evening?" If they could not solve it, the Sphinx would kill them. Oedipus, who was a very intelligent man, solved the riddle. The Sphinx killed itself by jumping off the mount when he heard the answer.

Oedipus quickly became a hero among the Thebians since he had freed the city of the dreadful Sphinx. In fact, they made him king because their king had been killed. Oedipus then did what kings usually did in those days and married the queen, who was a widow. They had two sons and two daughters.

The rest of the story, which is not well known, is that later the people of Thebes were ravaged by disease. They consulted the Delphic oracle and asked what they were doing wrong to cause this plague. The Delphic oracle told them that their king had killed his father Laeus and was now married to his own mother, the queen.

When this news was brought back to Oedipus and to Jocasta, the queen committed suicide by hanging herself. Oedipus blinded himself and went out into exile, where he died. Indonesians have a very similar story: Sangkuriang.

A kind of romance seems to develop in families. Myths such as this live on because there is a truth within the story. A boy's mother is the nearest female, and his feelings naturally go out to her. But soon he learns not to touch her lest a thing worse than death overtake him (sexual mutilation). He wants to do what his father does, and to some degree, he becomes his father's rival for his mother. Yet he fears to do what his father does: love his mother as his father loves her.

JACOB AND ESAU

The Oedipus complex can be seen clearly in a story as old as the tale of Jacob and Esau. Isaac, the father of these fraternal twins, was quite submissive and feminine. Rebecca, Isaac's wife, was quite dominant and masculine. The sibling rivalry between the two brothers was just as modern as you'll find in any home today. Isaac loved Esau, but Rebecca loved Jacob.

Isaac was dominated by his father, Abraham, who had ventured with his father, Terah, and the extended family from the land of Ur of the Chaldeans to Haran. Later, Abraham was strong enough to rebel against Terah and begin his faith journey, following his understanding of God's calling. He left his father, mother, and home, and at one point was willing to sacrifice the life of his son, Isaac.

When one generation leaves a heavy footprint in the sand of time, the next generation will tend to leave a light footprint. The following generation will again leave a heavier one. The dominant person (Abraham) raised a weak son (Isaac) who raised a dominant son (Jacob).

Isaac was overprotected by his elderly mother, Sarah. In fact, Isaac was chided by his half-brother Ishmael for being a mama's boy because of his delayed weaning. Later as an adult, Isaac accepted as his wife the woman who was chosen for him by his father's servant. When he first saw Rebecca, he considered her as a comfort to him for the loss of his recently deceased mother. Isaac was looking not so much for a wife as for a mother. He wanted to replace his overprotective mother who had just died.

Rebecca was an active shepherdess who was aggressive about welcoming strangers, even strange men at the well. Her father had to seek her consent for the marriage. That was unheard-of in those days. She ran her family and planned for her favorite, Jacob, to become the major recipient of the inheritance even though it included deceiving her husband.

Now these two boys might have been equally loved by both parents, but instead, because of the parent's problems, the parents projected onto their sons compensations for their own frustrations. Submissive Isaac loved what he saw in Esau: the freedom of the hunter, because he was never allowed to do that in growing up overprotected by his aging mother. Aggressive Rebecca liked Jacob more because in his younger years he was easier to dominate. Each child was half-loved by his parents. Insufficiently loved by his feminine father, Jacob was filled with fear. Insufficiently loved by his masculine mother, Esau was filled with hate. Isaac's home life was unhappy because he and his wife were in conflict over what their roles should be in the family.

INFLUENCES ON PERSONALITY DEVELOPMENT

In this age of family romance, during which parents are usually seen as infallible, a number of developments influence the personality. The second moral sense develops in this period. It is positive and affirmative: "Yes, I can. I will," unlike the earlier, first moral sense, which was negative: "No, I won't." It is important to learn the meaning of no, so you can learn the meaning of yes: "I want to be good."

In this period, guilt feelings become a problem: the guilty fear of being punished for saying no and yes or the guilty fear of deserving to be punished. That is the kind of emotion the conscience has at its disposal to whip us into shape. Speech problems such as stuttering may develop due to the anxiety and guilt aroused during the age of family romance.

It is important that one parent does not do all the disciplining. The best way to discipline children is to reward what you like about their behavior and ignore what you don't like. Most parents do just the opposite. They ignore what they like and punish what they don't like. Ignoring a child is punishment because children want parental attention so badly. But if parents ignore good behavior because they expect it, kids will learn to misbehave to get attention, albeit negative attention. If punishment, such as a spanking, is administered, be gentle and do it only as a last resort, with the hand, immediately after the disobedience. One whack is usually sufficient. "Time out" is an effective form of discipline. The parent requires the disobedient child to sit still and be quiet for a brief period of time (usually about one minute per year of age).

Masturbation is a common occurrence at this age. Children explore their genital organs and find them pleasurable to touch. Parents become very disturbed about this, worrying about what some neighbor or relative will say about their child. Probably it is best to ignore it and try to be more relaxed about it.

Children also have a lot of sexual questions. They don't want a long scientific answer. They simply want to know where babies come from. After that, they're on their way to play, no problem.

There are some good books on sex education for children, which they can understand at this age. They are published in the format of children's books with drawings on every page and large print (Andry and Schepp, 1968; Sheffield, 1972). Parents can read these to their children and discuss them as they do with other books. A lot of parents make a big mistake by not talking to their children about their sexual questions. If you start at this age, then it is not a problem later when they are teenagers.

Another problem is enuresis, which is the word the doctor uses for bedwetting. This should not be considered a problem until beyond the third year. Bedwetting is more common among boys than girls. Parents are usually patient with this problem during the age of family romance.

Encopresis means excreting in the clothing. Usually, it occurs because children don't stop playing soon enough to get to the bathroom in time. They feel omnipotent and have not yet accepted their human time limitations. But that may not be the only reason. I will discuss enuresis and encopresis more in the next stage of life. In this stage, parents typically tolerate either problem.

Temper tantrums are another problem in this age group. Children lie on the floor, scream, and kick their feet. Some may even bang their heads on the floor. They usually resort to self-destruction that hurts themselves more than anyone else. When your child does that, leave the room. Don't stand around watching any behavior that you do not approve, or say anything about it. The parent who gets excited and tries to make the child stop, gives the child a lot of attention. That reaction reinforces the temper tantrum, and the child will repeat this behavior. But if you ignore the tantrums, they will tend to go away.

If there is a divorce when the child is in this age period, the child will probably feel responsible. When you think about what is going on psychologically at this time, it is understandable that children often feel that they caused a divorce. The little boy is kind of in love with his mother, and the little girl is sort of in love with her father. They have feelings of competition with the parent of the same gender for the parent of the opposite gender. Thus, children feel a ton of guilt, especially from the loss of a parent of the same sex, that is probably going to bother them the rest of their lives.

Death is a similar situation. At this early age, children can't understand death very well anyway. They have experienced people going away or going to sleep, but they come back or wake up. Children can't think abstractly enough to comprehend the finality of death. They don't know what causes death and think about it magically. They think it is because of something they have wished for or done (Fraiberg, 1959, p. 46). They may think that God is punishing them for their feelings or behavior by taking away a parent.

If children are not allowed to go to the funeral, they feel left out. They are not allowed to be in the family group. They see that the adults around them are sad and crying, grieving, but they are excluded from this. On the other hand, I don't think children should be forced to touch or kiss the dead body. If they go to the funeral home and they want to look at the body, they ought to be held up where they can see it. They certainly ought to be included in the conversation so they can learn how to talk about dying, death, and funerals. This all helps children to learn to treat death as a natural event.

Surgery is another problematic area for a child in this age group. Children become very frightened about surgery. They fear mutilation. I am glad that tonsillectomies are not performed as often as they used to be. Any kind of surgery that has to with the genital area of the body ought to be postponed, if at all possible, until a later age. If not, the child needs to know beforehand exactly what the doctor is going to do.

Another circumstance I have yet to mention is the birth of a sibling. This is a problem for a child at any age. If the child is included in planning for the new baby, then some of the problems are solved. Pregnancy is the natural time for sex education. Invite the child to go to the hospital and help bring mother and baby home. Encourage the older siblings to take visitors to see the baby. Let them have a part in the limelight so that they are getting some attention as they show off this new brother or sister. Breast-feeding will call for repeated explanations or a three- to six-year-old is not going to understand it. Children fear being replaced by the sibling or becoming unloved or less loved. The child is likely to resent or feel jealous of the attention that the baby gets from Mother, including the closeness of their bodies. Hugging and holding from both parents will help to diminish these feelings. It will help big brother or sister to be more relaxed and understand why Mother has to spend all this time with the baby, and it doesn't mean that she loves him or her less.

It is not surprising that little children often learn to fear animals. They look many dogs right in the eye because some dogs are as big as they are. We have to learn all of our fears except the two mentioned in a previous chapter: falling and loud noises. Since animals seem comparatively much larger to children than to adults, children need help to learn which animals to trust and which ones they cannot trust. They fear imaginary creatures, some of which are in their dreams.

I remember when I was in this age category, my grandparents had chickens, and to get to the outdoor privy, we had to walk through the chicken yard. Once, as I was exploring the world, I had picked up a couple of chicks. I was really enjoying these chicks until the mother hen came running up and flogged me. She was about as big as I was. She jumped and flew into my face, hit me with her wings, pecked me, and scratched me with her feet. She knocked me down in the process. For a long time after that, I was scared to death to go down to the privy. Finally, in desperation and at full speed, I would make it. Then, as I would sit there taking care of business, the chickens would seem to walk by looking at me with one eye, daring me to try to escape.

I also had a dream around this time that I still remember, about a pig chasing me. That pig still seems as real as a live pig.

Remember the castration complex I mentioned earlier. Children really do fear that they might be injured or mutilated. Parents get angry and say, "You do that again and I'll knock your head off." Children take that literally and can visualize their heads rolling along the ground.

Children fear being deserted by their parents. If this happens through a divorce, separation, or death, the child may never be able to have close relationships. Children can be helped to become bonded or attached to another adult, but it takes a lot of time, patience, and attention from the new adult. Children left at nursery school or with a baby-sitter need to hear the phrase "we'll be back" from their parents. Children at this age need the repetition. Have you noticed, for example, that they don't pay much attention to programs on television? They watch the advertisements. They like the repetition of something familiar that they've seen before. They'll come running in from all parts of the house to see a commercial. After it is over, they leave. They like the routine; it is stability for them. When the familiar parental figures are gone or out of sight, stability is gone.

Sexual perversions usually start in this age period. Exhibitionism is showing one's body, especially the genitals, to others. The flasher, almost always a male, exposes his genitals to unsuspecting women or girls. Children expose their genitals to each other in playing "house" or "doctor" to determine the difference between boys and girls. Psychologically, people who enjoy being in the public eye such as teachers, preachers, and politicians may also have exhibitionistic tendencies. This may be some of the unconscious motivation for choosing one of these vocations.

Masochism is the wish to receive pain. Some psychologists think that ministers are masochists. They put themselves in the position of trying to please everybody as the pastor of a congregation. They have a lot of pain inflicted upon them emotionally by one person or another in every congregation, no matter how hard the pastor tries. Ministers work hard, put in long hours, and receive small salaries. The masochist can't really enjoy sex or reach an orgasm without feeling pain. Such people may feel very guilty about anything sexual, so they need to have pain to get enough release from guilt to experience an orgasm.

"Infantile amnesia" is a term used to explain why we remember so little from our first six years. I wonder it if isn't related to an underdeveloped neurological system. We do forget and repress much that happens before we started school. We can remember some significant things (I illustrated previously a couple of my early memories). Some people can remember a few things as early as the third or even the second year of life.

Few people get through this age of family romance without accumulating the guilt of having committed adultery and murder. Children wish to commit adultery with the parent of the opposite sex and murder of the parent of the same sex. This is the age that produces much of our lifelong guilt. God forgives us and delivers us from this guilt later on when we are able to experience what we call a religious conversion. The gospel that we preach should communicate God's love way back into the forgotten, repressed material from the first six years. Incest, rape, adultery, and murder were really not committed but the omnipotent, magical childhood wishes occurred, and the guilt is there as though it happened. The gospel of God's love needs to reach deeply into the heart and memory to dispel this guilt.

Chapter 5

The Age of Friendships:
Six to Ten Years

Sigmund Freud named the period from ages roughly six to ten "The latency period" because from his psychosexual viewpoint, less sexuality is being expressed during this age span. Kegan (1982) describes the self that correlates roughly with this stage as the empirical self, since the child longs for independence and competence. Fowler (1987, pp. 61-63) wrote that children this age, who can now distinguish clearly between reality and make-believe, develop a mythic-literal faith (see Table 5.1). The need for compeers (Sullivan, 1953) ushers in this period. I call it the age of friendships. In this period of life the need for friends comes to the attention of the child.

TABLE 5.1. Stages of Faith

FOWLER		McCULLOUGH	WESTERHOFF
Stage 1	Intuitive-Projective Faith	The Innocent	Experienced Faith
Stage 2	Mythical-Literal Faith	The Literalist	Experienced Faith
Stage 3	Synthetic-Conventional Faith	The Loyalist	Affiliative Faith
Stage 4	Individuative-Reflective Faith	The Critic	Searching Faith
Stage 5	Conjunctive Faith	The Seer	Owned Faith
Stage 6	Universalizing Faith	The Saint	Owned Faith

Up to this time in life, the age of about five or six, the culture has been transmitted to the child by as few as half a dozen people: parents, older siblings, and perhaps grandparents, or a few relatives and family friends. The child has been given the familial view of the world, life, and other people in society. Today's children grow in the same dimensions as did Jesus: in stature (physically), in wisdom (mentally), and in favor with God (spiritually) and man (socially) (Luke 2:52).

Now the child begins to leave home for six hours or more each day to be regularly exposed to people in the outside world. The child has assumed that values taught at home are absolute and universal. Now the school introduces relativism. The school experience will confirm what the family has said that is generally thought to be true and will correct some of the errors in judgment that the family has taught. This may give the child a different viewpoint altogether. In the school experience, the person who now begins to loom large in the life of the child and will continue to do so for the next several years is the teacher. A number of things begin to be rather different.

Competition with one's peers now becomes serious. So far the child has usually competed with siblings who were older or younger (except for twins) unless there happened to be someone in the neighborhood who was the same size. Competition before was never quite fair anyway. If children played with younger brothers and sisters and won the game, it was no big deal; bigger children were expected to win. If children played with older brothers and sisters and won the game, it was no big deal because they let you win. Moreover, prior to school age the child was really too egocentric to actually enter into competition. In nursery school and Sunday school, for instance, other children were merely tolerated. Now the child's attitude toward peers changes and they become important.

The child also begins to learn that it is sometimes necessary or at least best to compromise. The child who finds out that he can actually outrun everybody in class decides that sometimes it is best to let the person he wants as a friend outrun him. Or the child who usually finishes tests first sometimes waits to let a few others turn in their papers first so they won't tease her about being smart or an egghead.

Children also learn how to get recognition, which builds self-esteem and a sense of worth. As adults, some of us choose our vocations partly because of the amount of recognition they offer. It feels good. Some children find they can get recognition by being bright. If they work harder and become smarter, they get attention from the teacher and their parents. Others find that they can get attention by being popular. They know how to get along with peers in the class- room and to get people to like them by being helpful or telling a lot of jokes. Being athletic is another way to get attention: run fast, jump high, throw the ball straight, hit the ball, catch the ball. Some learn how to do favors. Others learn how to please the teacher and become one of the teacher's favorites. But self-esteem is not a fixed attribute. It fluctuates according to the turmoil of life.

DEVELOPMENTAL TASKS

Children try to master a number of developmental tasks or behav- ioral objectives as they move through the age of friendships (Havig- hurst, 1972). I will mention Havighurst's work several times as we move through the lifeline. One developmental task that children deal with during this period is learning physical skills: basic things such as how to button a shirt. Some children begin school and discover that when their shirt comes undone they don't know how to button it. Preschool teachers will help children learn such things. But first- grade teachers simply refuse to tie shoes or they would be tying shoes all day. So, they insist that children learn how to tie their own shoes. It takes some physical manipulation to teach those little fin- gers to hold big pencils and learn to print or learn to draw or color inside the lines. There are several of these tasks, for example, zipping and unzipping pants. After nursery school, the teacher doesn't like to do that. Boys and girls have to learn this skill themselves.

A second developmental task is gaining wholesome attitudes to- ward oneself. Because children are out of the home now, six hours or more a day, they have to be able to carry a confident attitude with them out of the home to school. Mom and Dad may have taught this child self-acceptance and optimism. If so, it is not going to be much of a problem except that the child must be able to carry enough out of the home to last six hours. For some children who haven't gotten much positive feedback from the parents, that can be a real problem. It is hard to feel OK about yourself all day if your parents don't seem to think you're all right. Yet, feeling that you can do what the teacher assigns you to do and having a positive attitude such as, "I'll try it and I think I can do it," is important to the successful completion of schoolwork. Children have to develop selective attention, delay gratification, inhibit impulses, plan ahead, and pursue areas of interest.

A third developmental task is learning to get along with people of the same age. This can be a problem. Now children are around people the same age and the same size, about thirty of them, so they can really begin to test and see how body and mind work in comparison to those who are roughly the same size and age. Nobody is best at everything, even though some children were always allowed to win at home. On the other hand, some learn how to experience success for the first time because perhaps in their own homes they always lost. Nobody ever let them win, not even on purpose.

The fourth developmental task is learning more definite male or female roles. This certainly goes on through this period. Boys are identifying with the other boys. They like to do things that the other boys like to do and try to dislike everything that the girls like. In this time of life those male-female interests are rather distinct. Boys and girls try to keep as separate as possible. Since the feminist movement, girls have received more societal permission to participate in so-called "boys'" activities. It really pains guys to have a girl baseball player on their Little League team who is good. And, of course, some of the girls are just as good as the boys. Unfortunately, boys have not yet received quite as much societal permission to enjoy "girls'" games such as playing "house" or playing with dolls. In many families, boys still have to do these things on the sly. These boys would be embarrassed to receive a doll as a gift at a birthday party. Thus they don't have the opportunity that girls have to practice parenthood in play.

Developing fundamental skills in reading and writing is the fifth developmental task. This one is so important that unless it occurs during this age period, it really is difficult to attain later. I'm not saying it can't be done, because many adults have learned reading and writing, but it is really a struggle. During this age period, children can learn another language more easily also. Although colleges do take reading and writing quite seriously, not every teacher knows how to teach it well. However, parents can encourage their children to read more. Families that read good literature aloud together as well as keeping good books around the house encourage reading. This kind of thing is contagious. Pastors commonly encourage families to read Scripture together; here is another good reason for that. Children who see their parents reading will follow their example. If they don't see their parents reading, and the teacher encourages reading, the children are going to ask why: "We don't read at my house, so why is it important?"

Developing concepts necessary for everyday living is the sixth developmental task. This is similar to the first one, but here the idea is health habits. Children must learn the importance of washing their hands before they go to the cafeteria to eat lunch. They must learn to keep their feet dry and to avoid sitting with wet feet all day even without Mom or the teacher telling them. It is important to eat right and to do it in a calm, quiet atmosphere to avoid overexcitement, which can cause stomachaches.

The seventh developmental task is the further development of the conscience. This has come up in every age group. In grade school, it is a matter of adding and comparing values outside the home—learning some of the teacher's values, for instance. The teacher will usually emphasize values such as promptness, working quietly, neatness, and being well organized, so that the moment that he or she gives directions to get out the crayons, the child can find them quickly. Orderliness and timeliness are emphasized again. Children are on their own at school all day and if they don't take care of their belongings, nobody will. The other thing is that now they can compare their values with their classmates. Some may choose to commit social taboos such as using vulgar language, telling dirty stories, lying, or cheating. In moderation, these activities may represent normal testing behaviors during grade school.

Kohlberg (1963) elaborated six stages of "moral reasoning." He believed that grade-school children are only capable of attaining his first two levels, which he called "preconventional." During the first stage, moral choices are made to avoid punishment. In the second stage, doing right satisfies certain personal needs and desires ("If you help me, I'll help you").

In school the question of what is right and what is wrong is raised again and again. Stealing becomes a pivotal issue. If somebody takes someone else's things, that is wrong. In the family, missing property is still in the house and the owner will probably get it back. But at school, if somebody steals something, he or she will take it home, lose it, or break it. Thus, stealing can be understood much better. Lying, cheating, and copying are other ethical issues that come to be understood much better.

Personal independence is the eighth development task. Examples of this are taking care of a backpack, coat, scissors, ruler, and telling parents when a child needs new pencils. Developing an understanding of the value of money helps with personal independence. I don't believe in giving children an allowance. I think it gives a false impression that the world owes them a living. It teaches them "cheap grace." I think, rather, that they should be paid for the work they do. During the school years, the most important work that children do is going to school and studying. School children are preoccupied with whether they are "smart." Many would rather be regarded as "bad" than "dumb." So, in practicing family therapy, I encourage parents to determine an amount to pay each child (and it should differ in fairness according to age) for homework brought home from school after the teacher has graded it. The standard amount should be for a C, less for a D, nothing for an F; more for a B and the most for an A. More substantial amounts on the same ratio should be paid at report card time. In addition, each child should be assigned one or more household chores to perform regularly. Payment should also be made for this each time it is done satisfactorily. This kind of "piece work" helps children learn the difficult lesson of working for wages. They can then be taught how to handle their money wisely but independently in giving, saving, and spending (and in that preferred order).

The ninth developmental task is developing attitudes toward social groups. In some schools, children join gangs as a way of coping. Clubs are also popular. Children learn to love their group and to hate or fear other groups. In this age group, children don't really like the opposite sex; they much prefer their own kind. Boys will have buddies and girls will have girlfriends. As they get toward the end of this age group, the girls will begin to get pretty interested in boys, but the boys couldn't care less.

Religious conversion often happens nowadays between six and ten. The Roman Catholic Church has established the age of seven as "the age of reason" and, therefore, the time for first communion. This personal change is the central concern of Christianity. It refers not to development but to transformation of life: "a new creature" (2 Cor. 5:17). This was not formerly the case. In the early 1900s, several studies showed the average age of conversion to be fifteen. Christian denominations such as Baptists that emphasize believer's baptism will want to be careful not to place too much expectation on juveniles to present themselves for baptism and church membership at an early age. Children love to please adults, but that is not what Christianity is all about. Before children are intellectually ready for Christian redemption, they must have the ability in their thinking to abstract sufficiently to discern the difference between heavenly and earthly father. Similarly, they also must be capable of differentiating between disobedience and sin. They must be old enough to have developed the independence to follow through on their Christian commitment, or have sufficient family support to do so. Table 5.1 compares the stages of faith of three theorists.

PROBLEMS DURING THE AGE OF FRIENDSHIPS

School phobia is a problem that may occur during the age of friendships. This may occur for any number of reasons, but it is always associated with a fear, such as fear of the teacher, of a fight with an enemy, of soiling oneself, of embarrassment. However, the primary location of these fears is often not in the child but in a parent, usually the mother. The child's refusal to go to school typically occurs at the beginning of school or following a vacation period. The mother needs reassurance about her fears and that her child will be safe away from her protection. When she stops talking about her fears, the child's fears will usually subside. The child should be forcibly (if necessary) taken to school. After a few such days, the problem will subside. School phobias sometimes call for a referral to a pastoral counselor, a child psychologist, or family therapist.

Some children have more trouble learning than others. One of the things that parents can do to help the child is to institute a regular time and place to study at home. Children need to have a specific room and table or desk designated somewhere in the house where they can study. This ought to be a time when parents turn off the television. This is the hardest exercise that some families ever attempt. The parents have to realize that the children's study is more important than anything else at that time. For awhile children may need the attention or presence of a parent sitting with them. Some parents, however, are not good teachers. They are not patient with their own children and quickly become angry. One reason parents get mad is that they expect too much too soon. Another reason is that children are being taught different theories of math, for instance, and it is difficult to help them. Children can learn to study with the TV or radio on; most older children do so. Bear in mind that when Abraham Lincoln was growing up, the school was called a "blab school." Students recited their lessons out loud, yet the children were able to concentrate.

The study period should be made as pleasant as possible. If the children insist that they can listen to the radio or TV and study at the same time, then the parents may be wise to go along with that to make the time pleasant rather than making the children angry every time. Making study a pleasant experience is highly important. In general, I think it is good if children come home and play for awhile, then eat, and study after dinner.

A problem that has been coming to light in case studies among children in learning disabilities classes is that some of them began to have learning problems after the death of a family member or someone significant to them. In their grief, these children were unable to concentrate on their studies. Once they are moved into LD classes, it is difficult for them to get out.

Thumb sucking becomes a problem in this age group. It often begins earlier, but is usually not of much concern in the age of family romance. But if children are still sucking their thumbs after they start school, then it is a problem. Usually the ridicule of their peers puts a stop to this behavior.

Enuresis or encopresis is more of a problem for older children. Parents with ample patience simply let their children outgrow these problems, but that may mean waiting until a child is eight to ten years old. Other parents call in the help of a physician, pastoral psychotherapist, or psychologist. Nowadays medicine can solve these problems for many individuals.

Speech disorders or problems with hearing or seeing may be discovered at this age. Professional help is always needed.

Disobedience in school is too often labeled "hyperactivity" and is treated with Ritalin. The description used in psychological circles is "acting out." The person is acting out inner feelings. Some of the inner feelings that are expressed may be manifested in lying, stealing, cheating, playing hooky or destroying school property, and also uncontrolled temper or moodiness. Acting out inner feelings frequently culminates in disobedience in school.

Withdrawal may be a more serious problem than some of the others I have mentioned. The withdrawn child has few friends. This may mean that a child who is not helped out of this withdrawal may be moving toward mental illness. The teacher may be glad to have one pupil who is not causing a problem. That child doesn't get much attention and doesn't participate in classroom discussion. Yet these children need attention. Others know how to get attention by acting out. Withdrawn children don't know how to get attention. They begin to fantasize a lot and to believe in ideas that are not real. They have no friends they trust enough to share these ideas with so they eventually believe them, enough to live by them and then they break from reality into autism.

Childhood depression and even suicide has doubled in recent years. No one yet seems to understand exactly why. But children's depression and suicidal threats should certainly be taken seriously. I think it is a sign of family disintegration. Professional help is of utmost importance.

Several fears are typical of children during the age of friendships. One of these is the fear of failure. To get an F, to "flunk" a test or to fail a grade are dreaded possibilities that concern most juveniles.

Children also fear being ridiculed by their peers. Fights occur over this. They also fear the ridicule of their teacher, parents, or siblings. A third fear is loss of possessions. This has already been discussed.

Some students threaten to use knives or guns, or fight after school. Children attacking other children does occur and is frightening.

Children fear sickness and disease because some students are absent from school for a long time and then come back looking different. Children don't really like to miss school for long periods.

Children in this age group also fear death. Before about age six, they can't think abstractly enough to understand the finality of death. But during this phase of life, they may experience the death of several pets or even people and learn that death is irreversible, and at least by the end of this period, that it could even happen to them.

Finally, divorce of the parents is feared. Some of their class-mates' parents are getting divorces. They see these children every day. They know it happens. They also hear their parents arguing angrily at home, so they fear that their parents might get divorced. Parents don't realize how afraid of divorce these children are. See Table 5.2 for children's reaction to divorce.

This period is brought to a close when one chum or a pal takes on particular importance. Suddenly that person's views, needs, or wishes become greatly significant. When this happens, it is leading into a very close friendship. The children are not just playments but close friends. This brings one into the next era of growth and development.

However, before we look at the growing child's next stage of development, we need to think about what is happening to parents at the time these children move into the next age groupings.

TABLE 5.2. Children's Reactions to Divorce

Age of Child	Reaction of Child	Expected Problems	Risk Factors	Advice to Parents
Infancy (0-3)	Perceives loss of parent	Regression and develop-mental delays Problems with feeding, sleeping, and toileting Irritability, excessive crying Apathy, withdrawal	Loss of caregiver Diminished capacity of custodial parent Psychological disturbance of custodial parent	Maintain predictable routines Expect normal separation anxiety to be exaggerated Support for parent caring for self and baby Substitute care for infant if parent is seriously depressed
Preschool (3-5)	Fears of abandonment Fears loss of custodial parent Confusion	Whining, clinging, and fearful behavior Regression and develop-mental delays Nightmares, bewilderment, confusion, aggression Sadness, neediness, low self-esteem Denial, perfect behavior	Persistent or severe regression, nightmares, or separation anxiety Persistent encopresis with smearing Refusal of nonresident parent to visit or of resident parent to allow visits Inability of parent to enforce discipline	Both parents should tell child-ren about divorce and what is occurring Establish daily routine Maintain consistent discipline Emphasize that children are not responsible for divorce Encourage involvement of both parents in children's lives
Early school age (6-8)	Guilt, self-blame for divorce Sense of loss Feels betrayed, rejected Confusion	Sadness, crying, depression Longing for absent parent Anger, tantrums, acting out Asks for reconciliation Increased behavior problems	Developmental arrest, no new learning Loss of interest in peers and activities Other losses—friends, pet, relatives Changes in school or teacher	Regular frequent visits by noncustodial parent Shielding from parental hostility Involvement of both parents in child's care Consistent discipline Regular school attendance

TABLE 5.2 *(continued)*

Age of Child	Reaction of Child	Expected Problems	Risk Factors	Advice to Parents
Older school age (9-11)	Can view divorce as parents' problem but needs to find blame or reason Feels shame, rejection, resentment, loneliness	Conflicting loyalties between parents Worry about custody Hostility toward one or both parents Dependency School problems Increased behavior problems	Ongoing hostility between parents Complete rejection of one parent Parents pressure child to take sides Decrease in school performance	Involvement of both parents Parents avoid blaming each other Parental honesty Defuse child's anger
Adolescence (12-18)	Concern about loss of family life Concern about own future Feels responsible for family members Anger, hostility	Immature behavior Early or late development of independence Overcloseness or competition with same-sex parent Worry about own role as sexual or marital partner	Persistent academic failure Depression and suicide threats Delinquency or promiscuity Substance abuse	Maintain parent role with child Limit involvement in parent worries Child needs peer support Maintain consistent discipline Be aware of emotional ups and downs of adolescence—may be aggravated by stress of divorce

Source: Rakel, 1995, p. 41.

Chapter 6

The Age of Achievement:
Forty to Sixty Years

This chapter disrupts the flow of childhood development described in Chapters 2 through 5. Family systems theory maintains that development proceeds not only in a linear motion, but in a cyclical movement. Children and parents relate and interact, and this greatly influences development. Thus I believe that a discussion of what is going on in adult development as they are raising children is important.

People on average live much longer today than they used to. In fact, until about the middle of the nineteenth century, the 50 percent of people who survived their first year of life could expect to die between ages forty and fifty. They would barely reach this category, which is now often called "middle adulthood." Life expectancy didn't begin to change very rapidly until about 1900. One statistic that is often referred to in medical schools is that it wasn't until about 1916, after the Flexner report (Flexner, 1910), that patients had better than a 50 percent chance of recovery if they saw a physician. Prior to 1916, patients' chances were greater than 50 percent that they would get worse, not better. Consider how physicians treated patients prior to that time. They used leeches; they created blisters with hot suction vials; they did a lot of lancing. They used cathartics, emetics, and purgatives. They thought that if they could make blisters on patients, and cause them to vomit, urinate, and defecate a great deal, they could drain out some of that "bad" blood and other poisonous liquids or "humors" that made people sick. We know now that none of those things are particularly helpful except on very rare occasions. Physicians used to contribute to death and disease more often than they helped.

A lot is said about revering ancestors, but bear in mind that it was easier to revere and honor the aged when there weren't many of them around. Our average longevity is increasing rapidly. More and more older people are in the population. More than 25,000 people in the United States are 100 years old or older. This means that in this century we have greatly extended the time of adulthood.

As the children in a family begin to move into their teenage years, their parents begin to move into middle age. Thus, a family may well be in double trouble. Adults hope that life begins at forty. But a great many are fearful and anxious that it may end there. To the best of my knowledge, it was Swiss psychiatrist Carl Jung (1969, pp. 398, 399) who first pointed out (back in the 1920s) that people confront a genuine crisis in the movement from young to middle adulthood. He viewed middle life as a time of maximum potential for personality growth.

MIDLIFE CRISIS

The midlife passage begins in the mid-thirties, when people reach thirty-five and get to the actual midpoint mathematically of the biblical threescore and ten (which, interestingly enough, has been rather difficult to surpass in making life longer). Thirty-five is the end of growing up and the beginning of growing old. The literature indicates two things: one is that most people will experience a personal crisis during this time, the other is that those who avoid a crisis often become depressed. It is a little discouraging, either way you look at it, according to the literature. However, it should also be mentioned that many sociologists do not support the notion that most people will have a midlife crisis (McCrae and Costa, 1984).

Elliot Jaques, a London psychoanalyst, probably coined the term midlife crisis (1973, pp. 140-165) in a paper published in 1965, wherein he discussed the crisis in the lives of well-known people such as Beethoven, Goethe, Ibsen, Voltaire, and Gauguin. He studied their lives, biographies, autobiographies, and so forth, and found that the death rate showed a sudden increase between ages thirty-five and thirty-nine for 310 of these people with superior gifts. He also noted that their death rate dropped below normal from ages forty to forty-four and then returned to the average. Something important seemed to be happening in this midlife period, and it seemed to take awhile to get through it and settle back to "normal."

Middle age is a matter of perspective. In Neugarten's (1968) study the working class described themselves as middle aged at forty and old at sixty. Executives and professionals did not see themselves as reaching middle age until they were fifty or old until they were seventy. Thus, there is a sociological difference. The forties are the old age of youth and the fifties are the youth of old age. People view their chronological age differently in terms of their psychological age.

At about the age of forty, most of Levinson's subjects (1978) became fixed on some key event in their careers. They saw this key event as carrying a kind of ultimate message of their affirmation or their devaluation in society. This was seen by some as a job promotion, or a promotion in rank; for others it was a new job, or an award for publishing a book—some form of recognition. Most of them began to fixate on a future possibility such as this, which would be a communication from society either that they were all right or they didn't quite make it, one or the other. The outcome of this key event usually took from three to six years to unfold and finally happen. So, many forty-year-olds live in a state of suspended animation while they are waiting for this event to occur. They may try it only once or several times before they finally give up and accept the negative answer rather than waiting for the positive.

The midlife transition occurs whether the individual succeeds or fails in the search for affirmation by society. Life goes on and the person becomes more aware of a sense of bodily decline and a recognition of personal mortality: death really is closer than it used to be. A sense of aging was present in these subjects: an acknowledgment that they could no longer do all that they used to do. Also, researchers found a polarity of the masculine and feminine with an emergence of the feminine side of the self.

During the age of achievement, adults move into the era of genuinely wanting to serve others. They cease to be preoccupied with what parent figures can do for them and decide to become parent figures and mentors for others. Erikson (1963) called this "generativity." This means a feeling of voluntary obligation to care for other people. Having children, being a father or mother, does not necessarily ensure generativity. It promotes it, but it doesn't guarantee it; neither does childlessness necessarily prevent it. It is a psychological attitude of choosing to care for other people. Moving into generativity may be a frustrating experience as Harry Chapin's song "Cat's in the Cradle" indicates. Erikson and Erikson's (1982, p. 70) definition also encompassed procreativity, productivity, and creativity. It means becoming part of the solution instead of part of the problem and contributing something more than you found when you came along in the stream of history. Creativity includes assuming a measure of true authority and a willingness to become a model for the next generation. This includes acting as a judge of evil and a transmitter of ideal values.

Bernice Neugarten, in *Middle Age and Aging* (1968), said that men become more receptive to affiliations and the nurturing of others during middle age. Women, on the other hand, become more assertive and egocentric during this time and feel less guilty about it. This means that at just about the time that a man's tenderness begins to flow, his children are in their teenage rebellion and are demanding distance. The man is likely to be challenged on three fronts at once. He allows his emotions wider expression just when his wife is beginning to distinguish herself from him and wants to make some sort of mark in the world for herself. He and his wife pass one another like proverbial ships in the night; he moves in the direction where she has been and she moves where he has been. He reaches out for his children just when they are revolting against him. They no longer beg him to play in the backyard; they just want the car keys or money. He gropes for some way to become generative just when he is beginning to feel stagnant at work and maybe when some younger person is already on the job and being groomed to take over his position.

Most of the research into adult development seems to agree that the path to replenishment for men in midlife is through nurturing, teaching, and serving other people. This seems to be the best way for males to deal with middle age. However, this is what women have been doing all along. Around age forty-five the literature indicates that a man's life will generally restabilize.

At whatever age a woman knows that she will never have another child, a new kind of creativity is released within her. This includes not only menopause, but also surgical menopause brought about by sterilization and hysterectomy. She can no longer be creative in the sense of creating human beings within her body and teaching them, loving them, and nurturing them into adulthood. But it does release her from that responsibility and sets her free to try some other ways of forging accomplishments. Researchers believe that women can find their way through the midlife passage by transcending their dependency through self-declaration.

PHYSICAL CHARACTERISTICS

Physically, during the age of achievement, people generally enjoy good health. As they move through this age period, however, they may notice some changes. Their physical vigor becomes slightly depleted in comparison to earlier days. They may discover that it is more difficult to throw off some illnesses such as the common cold or influenza. They may contract these sicknesses more often, and they may last a day or two longer than before. Movements become less rapid, heart action becomes slower and less vigorous, lung action is weaker, and they begin to put on weight.

If obesity can be defined arbitrarily as weighing 20 percent or more above the actuarial insurance tables, then more than one-third of all adults in America between ages thirty and sixty are obese according to a study by the Centers for Disease Control and Prevention. Obviously, becoming overweight does not occur on purpose. But as people move out of adolescence, they continue to eat just about as much they did as teenagers and yet they get less exercise every year. Their hearts are beating less vigorously and so they gain three to five pounds a year. Not bad, except that if you do that for ten years, it adds up to thirty to fifty pounds. Many Americans become obese during the age of achievement. It is definitely a health hazard and it is sinful in the light of Scripture. Some of us used to preach against smoking before doctors discovered it was killing people, but I have rarely, if ever, heard any clerical warnings about overeating.

Chronic ailments, such as sinusitis, arthritis, hypertension, orthopedic impairment, deafness, allergies, heart disease, and chronic bronchitis often begin during the age of achievement. Around 8 percent of people in the United States are hypertensive and 4 percent are arthritic.

These chronic diseases, once acquired, must be coped with for the remainder of life.

Unfortunately, aerobic exercise seems to have peaked among Americans in the early 1980s. But many middle-aged people, sensing a depletion of their physical powers, begin a program of walking, running, biking, swimming, rowing, or cross-country skiing. Some use indoor machines to keep exercising during the winter. Such habits, formed in midlife, often continue into old age. Vigorous exercise increases strength, energy, flexibility, and perhaps health and length of life.

The so-called "change of life" comes in the middle of the age of achievement for women aged forty to fifty and toward the end of it for men aged fifty to sixty. For women, this is commonly referred to as menopause—ceasing menstruation. For men the word "climacteric"—a major turning point—is a better term since men never menstruate. Menopause encompasses three dimensions. Physiologically, the menstrual cycle ends. Sociologically, the empty-nest syndrome occurs. And psychologically, the people involved stop looking toward the future so much and begin to value the past. They begin to realize that some of the best things in their life have already happened and that they should stop sacrificing the present moment on the altar of the future so often (see Figure 6.1).

FIGURE 6.1. Life Line in the Age of Achievement

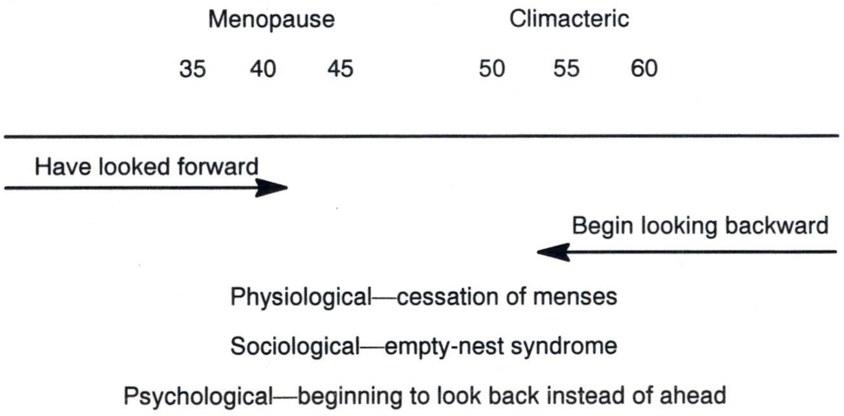

	Menopause			Climacteric	
35	40	45	50	55	60

Have looked forward
→

Begin looking backward
←

Physiological—cessation of menses

Sociological—empty-nest syndrome

Psychological—beginning to look back instead of ahead

Gail Sheehy has theorized that men and women are most alike sexually at birth and at death. They are most different around age forty. She calls this "the sexual diamond." It can be diagrammed as in Figure 6.2.

It has been well established that for men the production of testosterone reaches its peak at about age eighteen and that there is a slow decrease in its output thereafter until death. To date, the necessary studies have never been done to establish the true sexual potential of an eighteen-year-old girl. It is uncommonly clear, though, that eighteen-year-olds of either gender are fully capable physiologically of engaging in coitus.

Studies as early as those done by Kinsey and colleagues (1953, pp. 353, 354) established the fact that it is not until around age thirty or thirty-one that women reach their greatest availability for sexual responsiveness. Repeated studies have corroborated these findings. In contrast, after thirty many men lose their capacity for multiple ejaculations and find they must have a period of rest after an ejaculation.

During their forties, a number of men discover to their surprise and dismay that there are times when they cannot ejaculate once or even get an erection. This is often caused by the overuse of alcohol, which renders the mind more ready for sex but makes the body less ready. Some men say, "The first time I couldn't do it twice didn't bother me as much as the second time I couldn't do it once!"

For women, the decade of the forties is the most common time for the occurrence of menopause. The symptoms of menopause affect almost all women to some degree but only about 10 percent are obviously inconvenienced. Neugarten (1968, cf. Formanek, 1990) found only four women in 100 feared menopause, college-educated women least of all. Following menopause, women experience some combination of the following sexual symptoms:

1. Slowed production of vaginal lubrication
2. Reduced volume of lubrication
3. Thinning and loss of elasticity of vaginal walls
4. Shortened orgasmic experience

Men experience their climacteric during their fifties. Boston urologist Thomas Jakobovits (1970) concluded on the basis of four stud-

FIGURE 6.2. Sexual Diamond

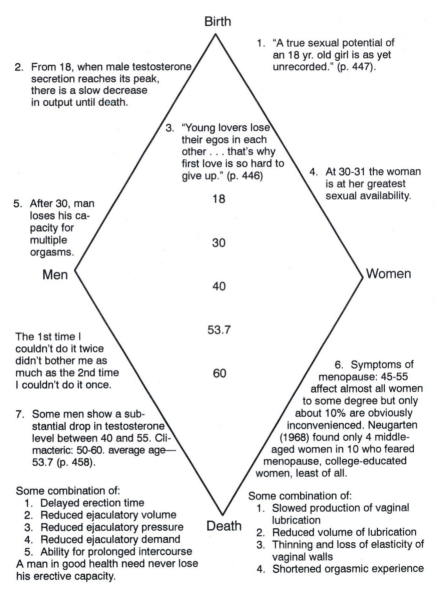

Birth

1. "A true sexual potential of an 18 yr. old girl is as yet unrecorded." (p. 447).

2. From 18, when male testosterone secretion reaches its peak, there is a slow decrease in output until death.

3. "Young lovers lose their egos in each other . . . that's why first love is so hard to give up." (p. 446)

4. At 30-31 the woman is at her greatest sexual availability.

5. After 30, man loses his capacity for multiple orgasms.

Men   Women

18

30

40

53.7

60

The 1st time I couldn't do it twice didn't bother me as much as the 2nd time I couldn't do it once.

6. Symptoms of menopause: 45-55 affect almost all women to some degree but only about 10% are obviously inconvenienced. Neugarten (1968) found only 4 middle-aged women in 10 who feared menopause, college-educated women, least of all.

7. Some men show a substantial drop in testosterone level between 40 and 55. Climacteric: 50-60. average age—53.7 (p. 458).

Some combination of:
1. Delayed erection time
2. Reduced ejaculatory volume
3. Reduced ejaculatory pressure
4. Reduced ejaculatory demand
5. Ability for prolonged intercourse
A man in good health need never lose his erective capacity.

Death

Some combination of:
1. Slowed production of vaginal lubrication
2. Reduced volume of lubrication
3. Thinning and loss of elasticity of vaginal walls
4. Shortened orgasmic experience

Source: Adapted from Sheehy, G. (1974), pp. 440-464.

ies that the average age for the change of life for men is 53.7. The most common symptom he found among his subjects was morning fatigue, lassitude, and vague pains. He found the following cerebral symptoms: nervousness, irritability, depression, crying, insomnia, memory lapses, apprehension, frustration, diminished sexual potency, and loss of self-confidence. Circulatory symptoms included dizzy spells, hot flashes, chills, sweating, headaches, numbness, tingling, cold hands and feet, increased pulse rate, and heart palpitations. The most bothersome symptom among his subjects was a decline in psychologic stability. Following their climacteric, men experienced some combination of the following sexual symptoms:

1. Delayed erection time
2. Reduced ejaculatory volume
3. Reduced ejaculatory pressure
4. Reduced ejaculatory demand
5. Ability for prolonged intercourse

For both men and women, the sexual symptoms listed above have been measured in laboratories. Individuals may or may not notice them even if their presence has been demonstrated.

Unfortunately, men do not usually learn until their fifth decade of life something that women usually learn in their third decade: that sex can be beautiful and fulfilling even without an orgasm. Men who finally allow their wives to teach them this important lesson usually find that they can enjoy sex without the pressure to "perform."

MENTAL CHARACTERISTICS

Mentally, the middle aged experience a period of continued creative activity. There is a decrease in learning ability of about 1 percent for each year after twenty-five. This is a slight decrease in the ability to learn new material quickly. People can continue to learn right up until death unless they suffer from a few particular medical problems. The maxim "use it or lose it" does certainly apply to learning ability. Those who use their learning ability can continue to have it right into old age, but those who stop trying to learn new things are stuck with what they learned in their youth.

People between thirty-five and fifty-five generally continue to learn, read, think, write, grapple with new ideas, and discuss them. Accuracy of knowledge and facts generally improves up to age fifty because of the wider accumulation of experience. These people have had more than just one experience that leads them to believe something to be true. Earlier they may have based a belief on one experience or one book they read. By age fifty their knowledge has broadened and deepened. There is a growing feeling of competence, confidence, and self-reliance on their own judgment, which is rather nice. It makes midlifers feel that they are finally getting to the place where they always wanted to be and thought would come much earlier in adulthood. They can trust their own opinions more than those of others. In other words, they have validated their own authority and the ideals and values they have lived by for forty or fifty years. This tends to make people less motivated to learn new things.

We need to acknowledge that for some persons this is a time of extreme mental strain, worry, or anxiety that may result in depression, insanity, or suicide. Suicide actually occurs most frequently among men forty years of age and older, especially if they have a health problem or if someone in their family has committed suicide.

SOCIAL CHARACTERISTICS

Social characteristics of people in this age group are also interesting. They tend to be at the peak of their vocational achievements and productivity. It is the age of achievement in their work world. They are not as likely to be promoted after age fifty-five. Of course, there are many exceptions to this generalization.

This age group participates more frequently in civic affairs. Any radical social outlooks of earlier years among these people usually become tempered, and they are likely to conform to a set social pattern. These habits usually go with them into old age. By the end of this age period, adults have had a chance to try out most of the things that they ever thought they might be interested in, and they have selected the things they like best. So they begin to concentrate on those things. They give up the idealism of their twenties for the reality of their forties.

People in their forties tend to reevaluate their adolescent conflicts and earlier choices about three things in particular: mate, education, and vocation. Among those few in their forties who have never married, many will finally commit to marriage. Many forty-year-olds get divorced and remarry. Many, especially women, go back to school, or change their vocations.

Generally it is during this period that the parents of these adults get old enough to retire and may have financial problems. They may develop serious illnesses or die. Thus, these achievers are in the middle again, this time between the generation ahead of them (parents) and the generation behind them (adolescents). Both these generations may lean on the achievers for advice or emotional or financial support. A movie starring Gene Hackman, *I Never Sang for My Father* (1970), is a good example of this situation.

Research studies show a slight climb in marital satisfaction during the last five to ten years of this stage for couples who avoid divorce and survive the passage of the midlife crisis together.

At the beginning of marriage, happiness is quite high, but with the beginning of the family it begins to decline. It drops to its lowest point at about the time the kids are in the age of adolescence and leaving home. Divorce is most frequent between forty and fifty-four (Sheehy, 1995, p. 129). The number of children in a family, of course, determines how long that time will be. That is when marital happiness is the lowest. Thank God, it begins to move back up after that. But a great many couples do not survive this low ebb in their marital history. The difficulties become too great and so they dissolve the marriage rather than weather the storm. Among those who remarry, about one-fourth are middle-aged. If they can survive it, things seem to eventually get better.

RELIGIOUS CHARACTERISTICS

The religious characteristics of adults during the age of achievement are interesting. Fowler (1987, pp. 71-74) refers to religious development in this stage as "conjunctive faith," which brings greater openness to encounters with the truths of other religions. He believes that this is the stage level of aspiration for the public church (p. 97). This is a rather critical moral period. There may be a noticeable moral laxity in business and marital fidelity. The woman during this age period may wonder if she is still attractive. She may not be sure that she can trust her husband's judgment, thinking he has to compliment her appearance because he is married to her, whereas some other man would only compliment her if it were true. Women know that in our society they are considered to lose their attractiveness in general as they get older. Interestingly enough, as men get older, find positions of status, and have an increased income, their attractiveness to women tends to increase. That means that both spouses have different kinds of pressure on them for marital infidelity during this period than they have had before. As you know, many succumb and yield to temptation.

Business dealings may tempt people to gradually change their values. At this age people become the holders of the wealth, the decision makers, and the ones in power. Sometimes that feels considerably different than it did when they were young persons looking at those older people making the decisions and setting or upholding the standards. There is a tendency in this period to drift and take spiritual matters lightly or become less visionary in spiritual areas. The opportunity for achievement in the business or social world becomes enticing to a great many, to the point that they may give up some formerly important religious practices to make extra money. They do, of course, have the financial burden of adolescents who are old enough for college, and college expenses continually increase. So, the sharp, idealistic line between what is right or wrong may for some be blurred by the realities of middle age.

While parents are experiencing middle age, their children are moving into and through puberty and adolescence. Those two developmental stages are what we will consider in the next two chapters.

Chapter 7

The Age of Discovery:
Ten to Thirteen Years

In psychological literature the period from ages ten to thirteen is usually called "puberty." "Puberty is the attainment of reproductive capacity" (Stoudemire, 1998, p. 298). Selfhood in this stage is called the interpersonal self by Kegan (1982). Fowler (1987, pp. 63-66) describes young people in this age group who can now do abstract thinking, completing a synthesis of values, beliefs, and allegiances that help to shape identity and worth. I think of it as the age of discovery. It is a very short span of time for some people individually, and it is not a very long period of time on the lifeline. But it is long enough for some very significant things to happen.

Socially, the way it starts has to do with the newfound, same-sex friend that I mentioned that closes off the age of friendships, where there are lots of friends but one friend is not much more important than another. It depends in part on who is available as much as anything else. The age of discovery is ushered in relationally by the newfound importance of another person. The best friend provides the possibility for experiencing more intimacy than the individual has known thus far in life. In this period of discovery, revolutionary changes take place in the person's attitude toward the world. Up to this time in life, the person has been extraordinarily self-centered or egocentric. Now the thing that seems most important to the individual is to draw close to this one other person and take an interest in the needs of another. This is not typical of younger children.

Generally, friendships are more stable in rural than in urban areas. However, so much mobility occurs in our society that a given person will have only a few friends in high school that became acquaintances as early as the first or second grade.

One of the reasons that kids in the age of discovery develop a best friend and have deeper intimacy than they have known before is the physiological changes that begin to occur. A sudden growth spurt, dramatically increasing height and weight, may occur now or later in adolescence. On the average, girls start their growth spurt two years before boys do (Levine, Carey, and Crocker, 1992, p. 65). For boys, this increase is usually accompanied by a tremendous appetite.

SECONDARY SEX CHARACTERISTICS

In this period of time, adolescents discover bodily changes that are called secondary sex characteristics. We come with our primary sexual characteristics, the genitalia, which identify us as male or female. But when we reach puberty, the second secondary sex characteristics develop. These are quite new and make a person look and feel different. One way those experiencing puberty try to become comfortable with all the changes that are happening to them is to talk about these things with one member of the same sex and try to understand.

You have noticed that the secondary sex characteristics usually begin earlier for girls if you have ever attended a junior high school (or eighth grade) graduation. In spite of being dressed up and on their best behavior, the graduates look like a mix of mostly immature boys and girls with some taller, rather mature-looking young women. Some of these boys will not grow taller than their female classmates until they are juniors in high school.

One secondary sex characteristic for girls is development of breasts. It is a kind of status symbol for a girl to wear a brassiere. It means that she is growing up and becoming a woman. Some girls who have an older sister will try to convince their mother that they need to start wearing a bra well before they get into this age group. The breasts have become such a fashionable body part that they really are a status symbol of womanhood.

Girls also develop new hair on their body: on the legs, under the arms, and in the pubic area. These are a status symbol too but most women in our culture are not very comfortable with this hair. They shave off hair on their legs and underarms as fast as it grows. In the

1960s, as part of the women's liberation movement, a number of women decided that this God-given hair did not have to be cut off. People sometimes ask me why I grow a beard every winter. I tell them that I am giving in to God's will. Every time I shave it off, it grows right back again the next day. God seems to want me to have a beard. Catholics often reason that whatever happens naturally should not be tampered with at all. It is called "natural theology."

The ripening of ova and menarche occurs during the age of discovery. The onset of menstruation now occurs six months earlier than for women who were born before the 1930s. The average age of menarche is about twelve and one half (Stoudemire, 1998, p. 298). That is not too hard to understand since children eat better and get more vitamins nowadays. Menstruation begins for most young ladies between ten and thirteen. Once it begins, it will occur about 400 times.

Throughout much of human history, women married shortly after they became physically adult. Their bodies were then ready to receive male sperm and produce new life. Nowadays, we don't even consider these young girls adults. On the average, when women were getting married around fourteen or shortly thereafter, they also were dying by forty. Women had their offspring early so they could live long enough to raise the children to maturity. About a twenty-year span is needed to raise children to become independent adults. Menstruation can creep up on parents pretty quickly.

It can be very traumatic for a girl in this age category to suddenly begin to bleed from her genitals and not understand why. In our society girls usually have received information about this from adults and peers at home, school, and church. They know about it, expect it, and feel good about it. It is a sign of growing up. These are the secondary sex characteristics that help girls to become young women: development of breasts, growth of new hair, beginning of menstruation, and the ability to conceive children.

The secondary sex characteristics start later chronologically for boys than for girls. They include the deepening of the voice, which is usually quite noticeable and embarrassing. We usually tease boys about that. Hair begins to grow on new areas of the body: the legs, pubic area, under the arms, and later on the face, chest, abdomen, and perhaps other parts of the body. The guys don't shave this hair except maybe a little off their faces. They feel good about this hair, and they want to show it the best they can. It is a sign of masculinity. They feel quite differently about new body hair than girls do. The last of these secondary sex characteristics is the development of semen and the ability to ejaculate. This also means the onset of nocturnal emissions or wet dreams.

Women have no nocturnal emissions, but they do have romantic dreams about men. For a male to be ready physically to perform sexually, he must have an erection. The corresponding readiness within the female is not nearly so obvious, but involves the lubrication of the vagina. For the male, the orgasm includes ejaculating sperm, which is caused by the throbbing of the prostate gland. Nothing is ejaculated by the woman. She is the receptacle. But there is, during orgasm, the rhythmic spasm of the vagina. There may be in women, although it is more rare, dreams during which the vagina has contractions for a few seconds. God created the male body to produce a certain amount of seminal fluid as well as sperm to be ejaculated. There is an accumulated reservoir of this fluid that is always in readiness while the body stands ready to produce even more. A physiological tension develops in the male to ejaculate some of this now and then. Thus, the male without a regular interpersonal sexual outlet will have nocturnal emissions.

That is the reason a man is usually more frequently interested in sex than a woman. God has created within men this physiological need to ejaculate. It makes men more lustful, which simply means more aggressive in meeting women that might eventually lead to lovemaking.

This leads me to say something which might sound extremely radical or even heretical. I don't think all lust is always sinful. God created it in us and some of it is a very natural process by which man meets woman and makes love. Nevertheless, it is easy for us to take potshots at sexuality and call all of it bad, morally wrong, and sinful. Yet God created us this way.

There is an interesting organ in the female, which is called the clitoris. Men generally do not know nearly enough about it. The only known purpose for this structure in the female genitalia is to enable women to experience the sexual pleasure that we call orgasm. I think it means simply that God intended women to enjoy sex. There was a time when nice women were not supposed to enjoy sex or, at least, they were not supposed to admit it. Fortunately, we have gotten beyond that.

Interestingly enough, all this means that humans are the most sexual beings that God ever created. The human female is the only one of God's creations that is sexually available to her mate at any time. Every other kind of female is only available at certain times. Yet the Church has not always been comfortable with that. In much of Church history, sex was thought to be sinful except for procreation. But we changed our minds. We in the Church have decided we were wrong about that, and we have been big enough to admit it. Now we say there are several good and appropriate reasons for sex. (I will discuss this more fully in Chapter 8.)

Unfortunately in some respects, this all means that children between ten and thirteen are able to perform sexually. They begin to have sexual urges just as strong as those of any adult. And these days more and more of them begin overt sexual practices. This is quite an issue for the Church. Children in this age group who are beginning to discover the delights of sexual feelings are taught by the Church that they should wait, not just a year or two, but about ten years. In other words: "Wait until you are twice as old as you are now." This is almost beyond their comprehension and many choose not to wait. Many Christian adults play ostrich and stick their heads in the sand of idealism, saying Christian young people will resist sexual temptation. But at the Family Practice Center where I worked, we have had at least one girl in this age category pregnant at any given time for two dozen years.

These kids are going to feel guilty about their sexual discoveries, desires, and activities. I think there is a lot of guilt. I see signs of guilt such as free-floating anxiety, nervousness, sleeplessness, upset stomach, and psychosomatic ailments, which are caused by emotional problems, not physical problems. However, this is not conscious guilt. People deny it or are not aware of it.

All these new bodily developments may give some of these kids feelings of personal omnipotence. Girls discover breast power and shape power, which will attract the attention of older boys and even men. Boys discover penis power—the delivery of heretofore unknown pleasure along with life-giving semen, which denotes the possibility of siring children.

Once girls pass through puberty, they may become quite interested in guys and very aggressive about talking to boys or talking about boys to their female friends. They become aggressive about telephoning boys, who have trouble figuring out why the girls have suddenly become interested in them. Boys are still in their exclusive clubs and the only thing they want from girls is to be away from them. There is real puzzlement when the girls are already through puberty and the boys are not. Socially, this period comes to a close when one of the members of the opposite sex is perceived to be far more attractive than previously noticed.

Although fathers and mothers of children in this age group may become concerned with the emerging evidence of bodily adulthood in their kids, a time period which will generate even greater concern lies just ahead: adolescence.

Chapter 8

The Age of Struggle:
Thirteen to Twenty Years

G. Stanley Hall is generally credited by psychologists for coining the term "adolescence" in the early 1900s to refer to the age span of thirteen to twenty. Erikson's continuum for this time of life is "identity versus role confusion." I call it the age of struggle. After the discoveries of puberty are made, there begins a long period of struggle for the individual and the young person's parents. "Young person" is a good term for adolescents, not "boys and girls." When they look like adults, they want to be called something other than boys and girls. These young people are struggling with a number of things.

During adolescence, young people become able to think about the possible, not just the actual; to reason abstractly about love, religion, and the meaning of life. Many become idealists. Piaget (1977) named this ability "formal operational thinking."

One characteristic of adolescents is their gregarious behavior. They love to get together in groups with other young people. It's almost as if they acknowledge a kind of herd instinct. They don't particularly like to be with persons who are younger or older. They want to be with their own kind. The time they spend with friends is the most enjoyable part of their lives. They feel spontaneous, open, and free of adult constraints.

The issue of privacy is important to them, especially in connection with their rooms, their bodies, and their thoughts. They are involved in a seesaw between independence and dependence.

Adolescent individuals are attempting to find a pattern of life that includes the satisfactory discharge of lust. Finding out how others are trying to deal with this problem is one of the motivations that forcefully pushes them together with others of their own age.

Within their group they often have a confidant or best friend, somebody they are really close to. In the earlier ages, this was somebody of the same sex. Now for the first time it is often some-one of the opposite sex to whom they can readily and easily talk. There is sharing of struggles and solutions both within the group and with the best friend of the same sex as well as the girlfriend or boyfriend of the opposite sex. These groups become pretty exclu-sive. Once young people get into one group, it is hard to get out of that group or to get into another group. Young people are sometimes not in the group that they wish they were in.

All normally developing young persons begin a search for their true identity during the age of struggle. Erikson believes this to be the most characteristic task of adolescence and wrote a book on the subject titled *Identity: Youth in Crisis* (1967). He discussed identity issues in four major areas: (1) career, (2) morality and religion, (3) political ideology, and (4) social values. Settling the question of one's identity is a mammoth undertaking that usually continues into middle age. Thus youth experiment with various personality patterns, behavior, and roles. During these experiments they measure their thoughts and feel-ings along with reactions from friends and parents, trying to decide which really fits. They are dealing with a search for personal identity and trying to find out basically who they are: "Who am I? What can I do?" These are theological or philosophical problems that they are dealing with. Some of them get married at these early ages hoping that the person they marry will help them find out who they are.

Many young people try hard to identify with their idea of Christ. But one individual's idea of Christ is not necessarily who Christ was. Judas identified with Jesus so well that none of the disciples suspected the betrayal. I think that Jesus wanted us to be like him but in our own way. I think there can be problems in being overly identified with Christ if it reaches the point of trying to be Christ. I don't think we find out who we really are by trying to become Christ. There was a lady who was admitted to a mental hospital two or three years in a row right after Easter. I was assigned to do psychotherapy with her. She was so overidentified with Christ that she could hardly live through Good Friday and the crucifixion.

Søren Kierkegaard, the famous philosophical theologian, was so identified with Christ that he would not permit himself to marry his beloved Regina. He never thought he would live past the age of thirty-three, at which Jesus died. Age thirty-three can be a pretty hard year for ministers because we have such a tendency to over-identify with Christ. We know of the sacrifice that he made and some clergy offer themselves up to be crucified. Some church members are perfectly willing to help the pastor fulfill his ambition, symbolically at least. Thank God, the Church does not need another sacrificial victim. I think we find out who we are by being something like Christ, not by trying to be Christ.

Dating with all its problems typically starts in this age period nowadays. The trend is toward dating earlier and marrying later, which increases the time span of dating. Some guys are content to wait awhile to start dating. They get involved in athletics, mechanics, or some hobby and are perfectly happy without dating for several years. Girls get into dating a little sooner but they date older boys. There is approximately a two-year time lag in the psychosexual development of boys and girls, with girls obviously in the lead. Some parents push their kids into dating as soon as they reach the teenage years or even allow it in junior high school. Other parents say, "No, you can't date until you are sixteen." I think it is a good idea for parents to discourage their adolescents from dating for awhile. Negotiating the age to begin dating provides parents and teens with many opportunities to discuss dating behavior. It also relieves the teenager from peer pressure to date until an internal desire and readiness is reached. Dating, going steady, and how far to go sexually certainly become a large part of the struggles that go on within young people and between young people and their parents. These questions and other such decisions are actually most difficult for adolescents (or people of any age) to make but young people struggle with them in both thought and behavior.

Many young people even select a life mate during this age of struggle. I think that is too young for this decision in general, even though I married when I was in this age group and, fortunately with God's help, I am still married to the same woman. But I know statistically that is not the way things usually happen. People who marry before twenty are more likely to divorce than those who marry after twenty. That statistic has held firm for a number of years now. People who get married during the age of struggle are not very likely to make a good choice and may not stick with that choice. If both of them are beyond the age of twenty, their chances of staying married are greater than if either one of them is below twenty, and if both are below twenty, their chances are least of all. Fortunately, the average age for marriage in the United States has increased and is not in this age category anymore. Young people nowadays are not marrying as early as their parents, and certainly not as early as their grandparents. Most adolescents decide to stay single, at least until they are older.

Another problem in this age period is in connection with sexuality: the pressure to discharge sexual tension, to masturbate, or to engage in sexual intercourse. The Kinsey studies in the 1950s, the Masters and Johnson studies in the mid-1960s and 1970s and lesser-known studies as well, indicated that masturbation is a very common human experience in both men and women. Roughly 85 percent of women and 98 percent of men masturbate. People have experienced a lot of guilt about masturbation. The churches have condemned masturbation, and medical books published as late as the 1960s also accused it of contributing to several medical problems. If you look in the Bible, you won't really find anything about masturbation. Some clergy cite the story of Onan (Gen. 38:7-10) as biblical condemnation of masturbation, but masturbation does not occur in the story. Onan had intercourse with his brother's wife after his brother's death according to the Levirate Law (Deut. 25:5ff), but he spilled his seed on the ground. If you read that passage carefully, you will find the thing condemned was that Onan did not fulfill the Levirate Law. He did not enable his brother's wife to bear children who would carry his brother's name. Needless to say, clergy and physicians have condemned masturbation heavily, often calling it "self-abuse" and issuing warnings that it causes pimples, nervousness, sleeplessness, and other conditions.

Homosexual experiences are another of the struggles in adolescence. To everyone's surprise when the Kinsey studies came out, homosexuality was far more common than people thought it was. Yet it is not uncommon for young people who have had one or a few homosexual experiences to think they are irreversibly homosexual for life. Homosexual experiences occur as adolescents attempt to discharge their sexual pressures and curiosities.

I (Dayringer, 1996) agree with Masters and Johnson (Masters, Johnson, and Kolodny, 1986, p. 353) whose studies may indicate that homosexuality is learned behavior. I believe that genetics plays an influential part in the choice of a gay lifestyle. Human relationships in the family during childhood, such as overly identifying with the parent of the opposite gender, also help to mold a homosexual. This begins very early and is reinforced in adolescence to protect against the incestuous drive, which is the most proscribed and dangerous lust. The absence of the parent of the same gender in the family may correlate with later homosexuality. But, I believe homosexuality is a choice, a sexual preference, not a biological determination that one is locked into for a lifetime.

If homosexuality is a learned behavior, it can be unlearned. A few homosexual experiences may not define an individual's life-long sexual behavior. According to the widely publicized National Survey of Health and Social Living, only about 1 percent of women and 2 percent of men in our society has chosen the gay or lesbian lifestyle as their sexual preference, even though 10 percent is frequently given by the media (Laumann et al., 1994). About 10 percent of all the people I have counseled since I began concentrating on a counseling ministry in the 1960s have been homosexuals. Almost all of them have been beyond twenty years of age. If a person is well motivated to change his or her lifestyle, it may be possible with much time and effort.

Another thing that happens generally with teenage sexual urges is that they are sublimated. Sublimation is a defense mechanism, a way of rechanneling sexual energies into more acceptable forms. Adolescents become quite proficient at this. They redirect sexual energy into a more acceptable pathway such as study, athletics, mechanical work, Christian living, or sleep deprivation. These kids have an enormous amount of energy. They are not aware consciously of what they are doing. They only know that they have a great deal of energy and they get interested in something. They can pour their energy into activities that parents and society may or may not approve of and it drains off some of this energy that otherwise might be more of a problem to somehow use up sexually. For instance, I happen to work with medical students, who delay marriage later than any other professional group. They sublimate sexual energy into their studies. Protestant clergy marry relatively early. Roman Catholic priests and nuns usually sublimate successfully. What I am saying is that an average person can sublimate some sexual energy into studies, for example, and be a much better student than otherwise.

Some in this age period begin to have regular sexual intercourse with one or several partners. There is a growing tendency in this direction, a growing attitude among adolescents, in spite of what the Church and society have said, that it doesn't make sense, it doesn't hold true, it doesn't pertain to them, or at least they are not going to live by the rule of sexual abstinence until marriage. The adolescents that are maintaining their virginity faithfully need all the encouragement they can get. They come to church more often because they need lots of support and to see other young people who are also trying to live by this rule.

One of the big differences is that the triple threat that the Church and medicine have used for years to keep young people from engaging in sexual intercourse doesn't work very well anymore. The triple threat of infection, conception, and detection used to work well, but no longer. There was a time when syphilis was under almost perfect control; it is not any longer. Young people are engaging in sexual intercourse so frequently that venereal disease is again approaching an all-time high, but many of them assume it can be cured. There is one type of venereal disease that can't be cured. Genital herpes is a chronic and incurable sexually transmitted disease (STD) that is episodically painful and contagious. And AIDS has taken on epidemic proportions. But the threat of infection is not what it once was. There was a time when nothing could be done for syphilis or gonorrhea. Most people were truly afraid of infection. Doctors and preachers could remind people of this, and they took that rather seriously: "VD affects your mind, your wife, your offspring." But medical science has progressed to the point that the threat of STD is gone, with the exception of herpes and AIDS. AIDS is spreading to heterosexuals, and the fact that many people may not be aware that they have it for as long as ten years is claiming attention. The promiscuous are at greatest risk. The threat of infection should be heeded.

Most young people know how to protect themselves from becoming pregnant. So the threat of conception has lost most of its power. Contraception is very well taught; it is widely known and readily available. Some adolescents stay prepared and some parents encourage it. Christian young people, trying to live by the high standards of sexual abstinence until marriage, may yield to temptation and become pregnant. A Christian young woman may choose not to take birth control pills because she does not plan to engage in sexual intercourse before marriage. That is a real struggle for her.

The fact that birth control works so well and infection from STDs is supposedly curable make detection even less of a threat these days. Once adolescents became successful in obtaining keys to the family vehicle or to their own car, and even more so since they have access to enough money to rent a motel room, they stopped worrying much about detection. So, some young people rationalize, "Why worry? We can have sex without filling the world with children who have no home and no father—why wait? Detection is not much of a threat; even if I do get pregnant, abortions are readily available." When high school girls become pregnant, about 90 percent decide not to get an abortion. They will be accepted by their friends and will not become an outcast to her peers. We live in a different world from the one depicted in *The Scarlet Letter* (Hawthorne), in which a young woman committed adultery, was detected, and as punishment was forced to wear a huge letter "A" on the bosom of her dress for the rest of her life.

Another struggle for adolescents was long ago discovered in psychological circles—teenage rebellion. It is a very common phenomenon and can be rather healthy when it takes place in this age of struggle. Adolescents get into a struggle with their parents for freedom. Typical topics for conflict are schoolwork, social life, friends, chores, rules, money, siblings, and appearance. This rebellion occurs because parents tend to view their teenagers as being about two years younger than their chronological age, while the teenagers tend to see themselves as two years older. That four-year gap is a big enough discrepancy to allow a real battle royal. These family disputes are more common in early adolescence. Parental limits are thoroughly tested. Defensiveness begets reciprocal defensiveness. Adolescent egocentrism leads them to think they are more important and unusual than they are and to imagine that they stand before an audience that is attentive to their every word and action. Ideally, adolescents will learn that autonomy can be reached through peaceable communication and compromise. This may help young people to develop autonomous and advanced moral thought.

Teenagers are trying to determine what they personally believe. Parents have been telling them for many years what they should believe or what the parents themselves believe. But adolescents have reached an age when they want to decide everything for themselves. They want to exchange their secondhand religion or belief system for firsthand experience. The way they do this is to doubt what their parents have said. Often they have to say no before they can say yes. Teenage rebellion may focus on very significant things between the adolescent and the parents or it may center on inconsequential things. For example, the struggle with our two oldest sons focused on the length of their hair. That was the issue that we argued about more than anything. With other teenagers the significant controversial issues may be styles of dress, music, recreation, curfews, and even alcohol and drug use.

Kohlberg (1973) concluded that most adolescents reason at his "conventional" level, which has two stages. In the third stage of moral development, the individual tries to be a "good" boy or girl, striving to make choices that will conform to what the majority of people want. In the fourth stage, Kohlberg found a "law and order" fixation. Here individuals develop a rather inflexible attitude toward authority and laws. Adolescents have a more highly developed sense of personal guilt and social injustice. Kohlberg's "postconventional" level consists of a major thrust toward autonomous moral principles that have validity apart from the authority of the group. This level begins for some individuals in late adolescence. Thus, adolescents inevitably struggle with their conscience as they come to realize that society's moral standards change.

Faith often demands some attention from teenagers. It attempts to make sense of our everyday experience *"in light of some accounting for the ultimate conditions of our existence"* (Fowler, 1987, p.

56). It involves three kinds of understanding: knowing or belief, valuing or commitment-devotion, and meaning or story.

Teenagers are struggling with what vocation to follow as adults. Many of them begin to work at part-time jobs to earn money and to experience what it is like to work. The pressure to choose a career is intense. Some are unrealistic about their capabilities and aspirations. Some teenagers drop out of the usually expected track in favor of military service or to try a variety of jobs before settling into college or long-term employment. A few allow their parents to make these vocational choices for them.

Adolescents have several fears. One of them is the fear of being different physically, socially, and intellectually. They are also fearful of embarrassment and experience a lot of it. These fast-growing bodies of theirs seem too big to control. Girls fear being too fat; boys too short. After puberty, there is often quite a spurt of growth, and they are awkward. They really don't know how to handle these big bodies. They feel like little children and yet they have these big adult bodies. They also have many fears about the size and functioning of their sexual organs.

COMMON PROBLEMS

Identity confusion persists among adolescents. Yet, one issue that we are supposed to resolve in our teens is our identity. But few of us get that nailed down well enough to hold. It usually needs further placement and tacking for years to come.

Anorexia nervosa, an illness involving refusal to eat, is a problem for this age group. Young people die of it, and it is on the increase. It affects mostly young women, and very few young men. They simply stop eating or eat very little. A related illness, bulimia, causes them to go on eating binges. They might eat a gallon of ice cream in one night. But after bingeing, they rid themselves of the excess calories by using large amounts of laxatives or by inducing vomiting.

These young people develop a delusion about the size of their bodies. They think they are too fat when anybody else can see that they are quite thin. One of the significant influences is today's fashion of being skinny. Artists used to select pregnant women in their first trimester. They were the ideal artist's model: a little bit overweight and feeling womanly. Moving closer to our time, the artist's and photographer's models are thinner and thinner.

Delinquency is an interesting kind of problem that is confined almost exclusively to adolescence. The person who is delinquent may be rebelling excessively or acting out inner feelings. It may include skipping school, running away from home, or stealing, and perhaps even prostitution or suicide. The young person may have had some real difficulty in the formation of his or her conscience. Such a person may go on to become a sociopath or wind up in a reform school.

Schizophrenia is a mental disease, the most prevalent mental disease of all. It develops during the age of struggle. The admitting ward of a mental health center may look like a youth camp because most of the people there are youths. Schizophrenia is a faulty way of thinking, a breakdown in one's ability to think or to put thoughts together in ways that are reasonable and logical. Events take on strange meanings. There are four primary signs of schizophrenia: autism or withdrawal; ambivalence or unknowingly maintaining two contrasting ideas simultaneously; thought association defect, or moving from one idea to another in illogical or unpredictable ways; and inappropriate affect, or a facial expression that does not accompany the emotional tenor of what is being said. The most obvious secondary sign of schizophrenia is hallucinating: seeing, hearing, tasting, smelling, or touching things that are not actually there but are believed to be real.

Guilt is a big problem. A lot of the guilt is sexually related: guilt over sexual fantasies, masturbation, homosexual experiences, or intercourse.

Alcohol or drug dependence commonly begin during the age of struggle. In our time, junior high school kids are beginning to smoke marijuana and drink alcohol.

There are about 9 or 10 suicides per 100,000 adolescents. Suicide is thus not uncommon during the adolescent years. Suicide has doubled for adolescents since 1970, especially for males. The highest incidence of suicide attempts is among young women roughly below the age of twenty-four. The highest incidence of actual suicide occurs among men over forty. In general, women attempt it more and men accomplish it more.

The end of high school is a major turning point that places one on the threshold of adulthood. However, Sheehy (1998, p. 10) concluded that in the past twenty years people have gradually matured earlier physically and later emotionally. She thinks adolescence is now prolonged to the end of the twenties. People's choices shape the course of their development. The overall task of adolescence is to develop a sense of personal identity and positive self-esteem, to become autonomous and socially responsible, to enjoy work and play, and to be capable of making mature decisions.

Chapter 9

The Age of Conservation:
Sixty to Seventy Years

By the time people reach age sixty, the family who lives together has dwindled to two persons again as it was in the beginning. This introduces the decade of conservation. Sociologists sometimes refer to people in their sixties as the "young old." Erikson characterizes the sixties and beyond as "ego integrity versus despair." The word "gerontology," meaning the scientific study of the process and problems of aging, becomes appropriate. Geriatrics is the branch of medicine that deals with old age.

As people move into their sixties, there is a tendency to deny their chronological age, which seems to have increased so rapidly. My mother used to say when she was in this age category that it seemed as though she and Dad should be about as old as their oldest children, not in their sixties. Satchel Paige, an African-American baseball pitcher, made famous the question: "How old would you feel if you didn't know how old you were?"

Gerontologists have proposed three major theoretical approaches to understanding individual adjustment to old age. The oldest and most widely accepted is called the activity theory. This theory maintains that people stay engaged with as many activities as they can for as long as they can. Nevertheless, reducing activities in one area of life inevitably means decreasing activity in other areas of life as well. Thus, maintenance of activity levels is essential.

Disengagement theory is the opposite of activity theory. According to this understanding of aging, individuals purposefully relinquish their interests in various areas of their lives.

Continuity theory proposes that a complex interplay between individuals and society was established by patterns of their middle adulthood years. Some learned to integrate life's experiences and continue to do so by staying focused and reorganizing their lives as needed. Others reacted to their lives by becoming defensive or armored and continue in this manner, becoming more constricted. Some adopted a passive-dependent lifestyle and maintain their apathetic ways, becoming relief-seekers. Those whose lives were always rather disintegrated become more disorganized.

Projections about the percentage of the total U.S. population of people in their sixties expected to exist in future years are as follows:

2000	2010	2030	2050
21%	26%	32%	33%

Because of their greater longevity, women increasingly outnumber men in each decade among the aging. White males have the greatest probability of being married and black females have the lowest. As parents also live longer, long-term parent care has become more normal. Adult daughters provide 80 to 90 percent of medically related and personal care, household tasks, transportation, shopping, and so forth. Most family members feel some guilt about not doing enough.

Grandparenting becomes a new role for most of those in their sixties (if not before). A special relationship exists between children and grandparents that is qualitatively different from the one between children and parents (Madden and Madden, 1980). Grandparenthood provides a historical perspective on life and the family, and that tradition can be transmitted to the young, thus providing grandparents with a sense of continuity in their lives.

PHYSICAL CHARACTERISTICS

The physical characteristics of those in their sixties reflect the name that I have given to this decade of life: conservation. They are not engaged in as many enterprises as they were before, partly because they have less energy as well as less motivation. A little more rest is required, and yet rest is more elusive for many in this age period and beyond. People may experience more anxiety and feel that their nerves get upset more easily or that they have less patience than before. In general, a gradual decrease occurs in physical power. Specific weaknesses and ailments may become more pronounced. Somebody who developed a chronic ailment such as diabetes during the age of achievement has now had it for a number of years and may have had to switch from taking pills to using daily injections.

By age sixty, 20 percent of the men Kinsey and colleagues (1948, pp. 237-238) studied were incapable of sexual intercourse. At the other extreme, a recent study done by sociologist the Reverend Andrew M. Greeley (1995) found that 37 percent of married people over sixty make love once a week.

The most common causes of death in this age period are cardiovascular disease (39 percent), cancer (24 percent), and hypertension (7 percent). Because of the higher death rate of men, wives may become more concerned about their husbands' health than their own. They may monitor the health of their husbands to the neglect of their own health. The increasing percentage of the husbands of their friends and relatives who are dying in this age group cause women to be almost as afraid of becoming widows as they are of dying themselves.

Biology of Aging

Many physical changes occur as we age. Here are some examples (compiled by J. Paul Newell, MD, geriatrician):

Stature and Posture
- Kyphosis (curvature of the spine), postural changes, and flexion at knees and hips result in decrease in stature; greater in women; much of the loss is in the spinal column discs and vertebrae

Bones and Joints
- Most bony changes are of little consequence, with the exception of osteoarthritis and osteoporosis

Weight, Fat, and Body Composition
- Tendency to obesity; weight plateaus between sixty-five and seventy-four and falls thereafter; subcutaneous fat

distribution changes: leaves face and periphery and adds to abdomen and hips; net result is greater angularity
- Loss of muscle substance from 452 grams/kilo in the twenties to 270 grams/kilo after seventy; accompanied by a loss of water and exchangeable potassium

Body Hair
- General decrease, except on face
- Hair on head variable because of sex-linked factors
- Slow thinning; hairs less numerous and lighter in color
- Gradual loss of axillary, pubic, eyebrow, and leg hair

Facial Changes
- Muscles of expression cause wrinkles at right angles to the axis of pull
- Further changes result from loss of elasticity and sagging due to gravity

Skin Changes
- Wrinkling, dryness, tumor formation, hair loss, diminished immune response, and easy bruising; much of this due to loss of subcutaneous tissue, fat, and replacement of elastin by fibrous tissue

Heart and Blood Vessel Changes
- Gradual decrease in number of myocardial muscle fibers; replacement by fat
- Heart rate decreases/contractions are slower; cardiac output decreases; peripheral resistance increases

Lung Changes
- Damage to celia results in difficulty clearing secretions
- Stiffer alveolar surfaces; kyphosis and calcium in the costal cartilage decrease vital capacity and compliance

Kidney Changes
- Loss of nephrons results in impaired water regulation

Gastrointestinal System Changes
- Few morphological changes

Endocrine Changes
- Pituitary secretion unchanged
- Thyroid secretion decreases somewhat
- Parathyroid function unchanged
- Adrenal secretion decreases somewhat

- Estrogen production falls; androgen production continues
- Diminished ovarian and testicular functions

Nervous System Changes

- Loss of neurons, granulovacuolar degeneration, accumulation of lipofuscins, increased atherosclerosis, slowing of electrical activity, decreased efficiency, decreased sensory inputs, and diminished discriminatory capacity
- In spite of all, intellect is intact

Eye Changes

- Presbyopia, less effective rods and cones, impaired peripheral and night vision, need for more light

Hearing Changes

- Decreased ability to hear and to discriminate among sounds, decreased cochlear sensitivity, high tone loss, diminished transmission to the cortex, changes in perception and analysis of incoming data

INTELLECTUAL CHARACTERISTICS

Intellectually, people in this age group may develop a kind of impaired efficiency because of mental laziness. Factors contributing to this state of affairs include lack of interest, not being challenged by new ideas, lack of reading and investigating, and becoming more and more satisfied with answers they have already found rather than looking for new answers or being challenged by new questions. Verbal and reasoning skills as well as vocabulary, however, seem to improve in this age of conservation (Hoffmann and Paris, 1975, p. 435).

According to cross-sectional and longitudinal investigations, increasing adult age brings about some intellectual decline. However, different intellectual functions change with age in different ways. There is a decrease in memory, perceptual integrative ability, and speed on tests, especially nonverbal tests. People who performed relatively well when young will also perform relatively well when old.

Older people's interests in general tend to turn backward rather than forward. As people move through the life cycle, they mostly tend to look forward. One of the psychological aspects of menopause or the climacteric is that people begin to look backward. As young people we are always looking ahead. We want to grow up, graduate, get married, get started in a new job. At about the time of menopause (forty to fifty for women) or climacteric (fifty to sixty for men), people stop looking forward quite so much and saying to themselves that the best is yet to be and begin to realize that some of the best may already have happened. They find their minds turning back to the past more often than before. They tend to get greater satisfaction out of remembering the past than looking ahead toward the future.

Remote memory remains as good as ever. Recent memory suffers. A person in the age of conservation may have trouble remembering the sermon last Sunday, but he or she may be able to quote from a sermon ten years ago. Thoughts become rather well fixed, with less interest in new ideas. Changes and adjustments are made with more and more difficulty. It seems far better to keep things as much as possible the way they have been.

Yet for some individuals, this may be a period of great understanding and personal knowledge based more than ever on firsthand experience and less on secondhand learning that is passed on from somebody else. Remember the adage: "use it or lose it" or "the more we use, the less we lose." You *can* teach "old dogs" new tricks. The best professors may be in this age category along with the real philosophers, theologians, and historians. They have lived long enough to have a personal sense of appreciation for history. You rarely hear the word "wisdom" applied to younger people. Wisdom is more than just head knowledge of facts; it is a kind of experiential knowledge, tested in the fires of life.

This often is a period of economic concern with much worrying about the future. Retirement is coming up rather quickly. In fact, most retire or, at least, hope to redirect their lives during this decade. There is not much time left to prepare for this. If good plans were not laid down during the age of achievement, people may rightly begin to worry about how well they are going to live.

Among those who have remained married, home-centered living increases, based on a desire for security. People who may have divorced during the age of achievement are now remarrying in rather large numbers. Among those who remarry, about one-fourth are middle aged. So, many who remarry are in this category. One's mate is now more often seen as a valuable source of companionship. There are fewer new friends and old friends are beginning to be lost because of death.

The average family can be represented as a pie cut in the middle. Half has to do with the marital couple and the other half with their family (see Figure 9.1). There are one to five years before a baby makes the couple parents. Another slice represents the years that it takes for any other children to be born, usually including the preschool years. There are the school years: grade school, junior high, high school, college; this has a rather large share. Next comes the period of leaving the nest. The other half of life in the normal run of marriage is for the postparental years. I don't think couples realize this. A large share of life remains after the children have all left home and the couple are alone together again.

FIGURE 9.1. The Average Family

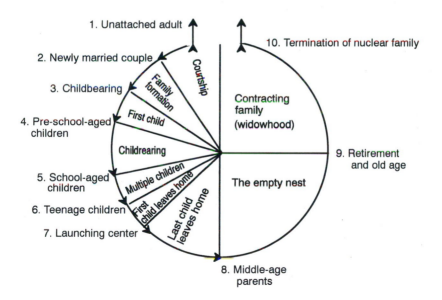

SOCIAL CHARACTERISTICS

Among the social characteristics of this age period, there is a growing feeling of inferiority in relation to the success of other people, a kind of continuous worry about being left out. "People never come to see us." People do not feel as important as they did earlier in life.

It is in this age period that people often volunteer to become mentors. Men and women are now beginning to see the end of their vocational careers, so they become more interested in passing on to someone younger what they have learned. They help some younger person to get ahead in the business or learn the ropes in the field.

It is a time for wider opportunity to travel. People in this age category travel more than they have at any other time in their lives. They can better afford it than they ever could before. They may travel on business. They may also be at a career level where they are asked to go and lead the conference, preach the sermon, give the paper, assume a leadership position. Also, it is a time of extensive contact with other people. The family is raised and more time is available, so these individuals or couples have time to move into the community and take on more active roles. They are good citizens who are more likely to vote than almost any other age group.

RELIGIOUS CHARACTERISTICS

Elderly persons have the highest rate of religiosity of all age groups. As age increases, so do the following measures of spiritual commitment: the influence of religion in life, putting religious beliefs into practice, and the degree of personal comfort and support from religion. Fowler (1987, pp. 74-77) concluded that the last stage of religious development is a universalizing faith wherein persons are drawn toward an identification with God, bringing about a new freedom with the self and others.

People in this age period tend to find it more difficult to change their approaches in Christian worship or Christian education. Sometimes when a new pastor comes to a church, one of the first things he or she wants to do is to change the order of worship. People in this age category can't see any particular reason for doing anything differently. They have been worshipping one way for years and it has worked reasonably well. Yet, young people, for no particular reason, want to try something different, just to see if it will work. This doesn't appeal to people in the age of conservation. They tend to follow the habits that are set earlier in life and to be rather happy and contented with those.

Those who remain in church in this age group tend to take on a renewed interest in some of the weightier doctrines in Scripture. They like to call their Sunday school the Bible class. It may be a golden period for some in Christian triumph as they look back and move ahead. For these people, it is a period of becoming more reverent, more dependent upon God, more worshipful.

For others, it is a bitter and remorseful time when they think about opportunities wasted. They start to develop an attitude that says, "I've served my time; let somebody else do it."

Most sizable churches have a Minister to Youth, but how many churches have a Minister to the Aged? Yet most churches have fewer youth and more elderly in their membership. A minister of youth must be paid, but I dare say that in most churches there is a retired person who has accumulated a great deal of experience and is qualified to serve as minister to golden agers, who would gladly do it without pay (or for expenses) if the church would offer him or her the position.

Although Americans in their sixties represent only a small (but growing) percentage of the population, they earn or have control of a good deal of the nation's wealth. They have earned the money to accumulate the things that they wished for in the past. Now they can enjoy them. Their past experience enables them to make decisions with an economy of deliberation and a minimum of frustration, and to make better decisions. They can do it better, more quickly, and with less energy.

Chapter 10

The Age of Retirement:
Seventy Until Death

Most people now live well into their seventies or even beyond, with the average longevity for women being eighty-one (Sheehy, 1995, p. 5) and the average for men being seventy-three (Sheehy, 1998, p. 9). Thus, most people do achieve the biblical threescore and ten years. While this stage of life is a part of Erikson's stage called ego integrity versus despair, I call it the age of retirement because people do finally and actually retire sometime during this period.

The population will continue to grow old because (1) the baby boomers are in their productive years, (2) medical science is improving infant survival and the length of life, and (3) people are having fewer accidents. However, it has been said that everyone wants to live a long time but no one really wants to get old. The following are some problems and some possibilities and gains associated with aging.

Problems/Pains	Possibilities/Gains
Health problems increase	Challenges to care for one's own body
Mandatory retirement	Retirement as a new chapter in life
Diminished esteem by society	Increase internal esteem
Diminished income	Stewardship of available resources
Future getting shorter	Living in the here and now
Time unstructured	Opportunity to choose what to do
Friends and spouse dying	Facing mortality and doing grief work
Old spiritual certainties challenged	Enriching/deepening spiritual resources
Confrontation with one's own death	Facing death in the context of faith

Adapted from a presentation by Howard Clinebell, PhD, at Laurel United Methodist Church, Springfield, IL, November 26, 1985.

Many elderly people have a resurgence of earlier skills, especial-ly authors, poets, and painters. Consider people such as Grandma Moses, Benjamin Franklin, George Burns, and Katharine Hepburn, all of whom were quite productive in their old age. At age seventy-two, former President George Bush parachuted out of an airplane. Tony Randall at seventy-seven, with eight Broadway performances a week of *The Sunshine Boys,* still was able to summon the energy to father a child with his twenty-seven-year-old wife. John Glenn at age seventy-six headed back into space, and octogenarians finished marathons. In Boston, a woman named Ruth Rothfarb died at age ninety-six after a twenty-seven-year career as a marathon runner that brought her national attention. She did not begin running until after her husband died and she was in her late sixties.

RETIREMENT

In 1883, Chancellor Bismarck of Germany introduced the idea of mandatory retirement, arbitrarily choosing age sixty-five as the retirement age. In the 1880s, only 2 percent of the population was over the age of sixty-five. Retirement was then and still is promoted as a reward, a permanent vacation, for the long-term worker.

Retirement brings about huge adjustments and requires changing the habits of a lifetime. Gail Sheehy calls it a "redirection" (Sheehy, 1998, p. 220). It means changing a self-concept that has been close-ly connected to one's occupation and relatively stable over a long period of years. It means changing a role that has been played for perhaps twoscore years. This may involve loss of status and almost always a reduced income. It causes a disruption of relationships with the colleagues and fellow workers with whom people have spent a large percentage of their time. Retirement brings isolation from the workplace and much more time at home. Boredom is a threat to the person who is about to retire. For some this occurs and for others it doesn't. Retirement may also usher in a time of identity confusion. Men especially have identified themselves with their work and have perhaps dressed the part through various uniforms or special types of clothing or hats. They may also have adopted a title such as mailman or milkman. Even titles such as mechanic or car-penter may have added to their identity. Women also have tended to be identified with such jobs as secretary, nurse, waitress, or house-keeper.

Retirement can be voluntary or it can be mandatory. My brother retired at fifty. My uncle said, "As soon as I reached sixty-two, I retired every few months." My dad said he didn't really feel retired until he reached eighty. Some are forced to retire with little notice, arriving at work one morning only to receive a pink slip with instructions to clean out their desks by the end of that working day. A considerable number of older people would like to work but have difficulty finding jobs, become discouraged, and no longer look for work.

Women who have not worked outside the home tend to already have adjusted to the retired lifestyle and all that goes with it by the time their husbands retire. On the other hand, women may not be ready to retire from their work as early as their husbands. Women often do not seriously begin their careers until their children have all started school or perhaps even not until the nest is empty after the children leave home. Thus, the woman may be reaching the peak of her career at about the time that her husband is ready to retire.

People have various attitudes and opinions toward retirees. I have been surprised at how many people have congratulated me upon hearing of my retirement. Others may feel that many of those who have retired have not earned the right and are simply lazy, leading nonproductive and wasted lives.

Retirement has a number of positive aspects. Those who are retired get to live where they want to live. Most retirees remain in the geographic area where they have spent most of their adult lives. However, there is a noticeable migration of retirees, mostly to the south (Florida) or the southwest (Arizona). Some choose to live in retirement communities that are architecturally designed and planned for elderly people. Here the age segregation enables these communities to plan activities that appeal to elderly individuals and groups. The communities are well guarded with fences, gates, and guards so that the inhabitants are much less likely to be victims of crime. Such safety features appeal to the elderly and relieve some of their fears. However, children and perhaps even pets may be rather scarce in these retirement communities.

Retirees also are able to do what they want to do. People wonder what those who are retired do with their time. The general population seem to think that television viewing is the number one pastime of the older group. Table 10.1 gives the findings of one study that reports the actual favorite activities of retired persons.

Retirees are usually able to travel more and also see relatives, children, grandchildren, and friends much more frequently than they could prior to their retirement. Also, senior citizens do a lot of volunteer work. In fact, senior citizens are usually the ones who deliver meals-on-wheels to the "old folks," that is, to seniors who are even older than the volunteers.

The past is a category of particular interest in mature age. By recollection, reliving, and storytelling, the acceptance of one's life is achieved. Gerontologists speak of this psychologically significant process as "life review" (Neugarten, 1968, pp. 486-496).

TABLE 10.1. Favorite Activities Reported by Retirees

Favorite Activity	Percentage of Retirees
Socializing with friends	47
Raising plants or gardening	39
Reading	36
Watching television	35
Sitting and thinking	31
Caring for other family members	27
Hobbies and recreation	26
Going for walks	25
Organizations and clubs	17
Sleeping	16
Doing nothing	15
Working part-time or full-time	10
Volunteer work	8
Political activity	6
Sports	3

Source: Dacey (1982), p. 312.

Senior Citizens Want What Anyone Else Wants

1. They want to maintain self-respect and personal dignity.
2. They don't want to be cared for; they want to be cared about.
3. They don't want to be isolated; they want to be integrated into the community.
4. They want to perform tasks within their capacities.
5. They want to exercise their right and responsibility to remain independent and self-directing as long as possible.

Some needs and problems of older persons are listed below:

Needs
1. Retirement in dignity
2. Adequate income in a rising economy
3. Suitable housing for both income and ability
4. Health
5. Meaningful activity
6. Adequate community service—transportation, nursing, doctor, etc.
7. Spiritual needs and resources

Problems
1. Too little income
2. Poor housing, high upkeep of older home, stairs to climb, etc.
3. Loneliness and feeling of uselessness
4. Malnutrition—lack of energy or ambition to cook and eat balanced diet
5. Having useful experience but unable to use it
6. Wanting job but no work available
7. Needing counseling for those and other problems
8. Lack of information on resources available, and lack of ability to get to them

HEALTH

The general health of those in the age of retirement continues to decline. This was discussed according to body systems in the previous chapter. Further problems arise as people continue to grow older.

The intellect does not change as completely as is popularly thought. Two prominent areas of loss have been noted. One is a gradual slowing of reaction time, which means it takes the elderly longer to learn new material than previously. As a matter of fact, this process begins in the mid-twenties and the loss continues from that age at about the rate of 1 percent per year throughout the rest of life. Second, the elderly have more difficulty with recent memory. Their remote or long-term memory does not change nearly as much, but they have more trouble remembering what happened yesterday or in recent times. They also notice blockages in remembering the names of people whom they formerly knew and sometimes specific words that they want to use.

Crystallized intelligence, on the other hand, progressively increases during later years. Crystallized intelligence reflects the degree to which an individual has incorporated the knowledge and the skills of the culture into thinking and actions. It has to do with what we often refer to as wisdom.

The elderly seem to spend more time in bed. However, their total sleep period actually shows no significant change. The problem is that the aging experience increased times of awakening during the night so that sleep efficiency is frequently reduced. Nevertheless, neither the amount of sleep per twenty-four hours nor the need for sleep each day decreases with age. Age-related respiratory impairment may account for a great deal of sleep fragmentation in the elderly (Birren and Schaie, 1985, pp. 261-295).

Sleep disturbances and sleep complaints are common in older persons. The prevalence of snoring does increase with age. My grandfather was a wonderful snorer. When my brother and I were small, while spending the night with our grandparents, we would often lie awake listening to my grandad snore. He had sleep apnea and there would be what seemed like long stretches of time when he would be entirely quiet. Then with a loud roar he would begin snoring again. We found that at times funny and at other times frightening, but always intriguing.

For retirees, the distance from death assumes more importance than the distance from birth. Introversion increases and role activity decreases. Senescing individuals find themselves yielding to a growing awareness that they are less competent. They yield their authority in the family. I remember how surprised I was when I began to notice that my father was giving up some of his authority in our family. These changes tend to support the disengagement theory mentioned in the previous chapter.

The elderly find themselves preparing or rehearsing a great deal. They rehearse for illnesses that will inevitably come. They rehearse for the loss of close friends and significant others. In earlier days, they went to professional meetings and read their alumni newspapers to find out who had been divorced. But during this time, they inquire of their friends and read alumni papers to find out who has died recently. They rehearse for dependency on others for their care, which they abhor thinking about. They rehearse for the disability that may come, requiring them to use a cane or a wheelchair, for instance. Furthermore, the elderly rehearse for death, and as far as women are concerned, for widowhood, since they often outlive their husbands.

Fortunately, retirees also celebrate a great deal. They celebrate the length of their lives. My father-in-law, the Reverend Jack Hymer Sr., said on his seventieth birthday: "God has fulfilled His promise to me of threescore and ten years; now I'm living on grace." They celebrate their achievements as they evaluate their past lives. They celebrate their experiences and relive them in their fantasies and thoughts. They cherish their memories. And human beings are fortunate enough to have what is called selective memory, so that we unconsciously forget those things that were painful and enjoy thinking about and remembering those things that were glorious and magnificent in our memories. The elderly also celebrate the heritage that they are accumulating to leave with their children, grandchildren, and larger family. Some of this may be their wisdom. In our country, we have not historically paid as much attention to the wisdom of the aged as has been the case in many other cultures. But now, with the ranks of the elderly swelling each year, the elderly themselves are seeing to it that their wisdom is being preserved for younger people.

Retirees spend a good deal of their time in what has come to be called "life review." This phenomenon is a process of reminiscing and putting one's memories in order. It may include designing and accumulating family memorabilia and arranging such items into albums and scrapbooks as well as using videotapes. It is a significant experience of organizing the various pieces of one's existence into a mosaic that has meaning. It is the evaluation of one's life with an eye to finding the meaning of one's existence. When this is positively and successfully done, it amounts to what Erikson called ego integrity. When it is negatively or unsuccessfully done, it amounts to the pessimism that Erikson termed despair.

THE VERY OLD

Sociologists have called the last years of life beginning at about eighty or eighty-five the "old old" or the very old. By the time many people live into their eighties, nature has found a way to pad them, in a sense, from the world in which they live. Those in this age category experience life as if they were wearing glasses with dirty grease rubbed on the lenses, with cotton stuffed into their ears, wearing shoes that are too large or too heavy to walk in properly, and with thick gloves on their hands. They find it difficult to get in touch with the world around them.

Touching is crucial to the elderly. Babies are touched during most of their waking hours in their early years of life. The elderly are rarely touched in the waning years of their lives. Yet they desperately need to be touched by their children, grandchildren, and friends who visit them in their homes, in nursing homes, in the hospital, or in the hospice. Physicians would do well to prescribe twelve hugs daily and PRN (as needed) to be given to the elderly by their family and friends.

Not until age eighty-five do over one-half of the elderly population report limitations in carrying out major activities of living because of chronic illness. The instrumental activities of daily living (IADL) refer to tasks required to maintain an independent household such as using the telephone, managing money, shopping, preparing meals, doing light housework, and getting around the community. The activities of daily living (ADLs) include such tasks as eating, using the toilet, dressing, transferring (such as from bed to chair), walking, and bathing. Better health among the elderly is associated with higher incomes and being Caucasian.

The very old utilize medical facilities more frequently and are hospitalized twice as often, stay twice as long, and use twice as many prescription drugs as those under age sixty. The rate of nursing home use has doubled since the inception of Medicare and Medicaid. Gradually, the social roles and responsibilities of being a child, parent, worker, householder, leader, and citizen are either removed or significantly changed (Whitehead, 1992, p. 159). The following vignette and poem demonstrates the plight of the very old.

When an elderly lady in a geriatric ward of Ashludle Hospital near Dundee, England died, it appeared that she had left nothing of value. The nurse going through her possessions found this poem.

> What do you see nurses, what do you see?
> Are you thinking when you look at me . . .
> A crabbit old woman, not very wise
> Uncertain of habit with faraway eyes.
> Who dribbles her food and makes no reply
> When you say in a loud voice . . . "I do wish you'd try."
> Who seems not to notice the things that you do
> And forever is losing a stocking or shoe.
> Who unresisting or not, lets you do as you will
> With bathing and feeding, the long day to fill.
> Is that what you're thinking; is that what you see?
> Then open your eyes nurse, you're not looking at me.
> I'll tell you who I am as I sit here so still,
> As I move at your bidding, as I eat at your will.
>
> I'm a small child of ten with a father and mother
> Brothers and sisters who love one another
> A young girl of sixteen with wings on her feet
> Dreaming that soon a lover she'll meet
> A Bride soon at twenty . . . my heart gives a leap
> Remembering the vows that I promised to keep
> At twenty-five now I have young of my own
> Who need me to build a secure, happy home
> A woman of thirty, my young now grow fast
> Bound together with ties that should last

At forty, my young sons have grown and gone
But my man's beside me to see I don't mourn
At fifty once more babies play around my knee
Again we know children, my loved ones and me
Dark days are upon me, my husband is dead
I look at the future, I shudder with dread
For my young are all rearing young of their own
And I think of the years and the love that I've known
I'm an old woman now and nature is cruel
Tis her jest to make old age look like a fool
The body it crumbles, grace and vigor depart
There is a stone where I once had a heart
But inside this old carcass a young girl still dwells
And now and again my battered heart swells
I remember the joys, I remember the pain
And I'm loving and living life over again
I think of the years, all too few, all gone too fast
And accept the stark fact that nothing can last
So open your eyes nurses, open and see
Not a crabbit old woman, look closer . . . SEE ME!!!

Anonymous

SEXUALITY

Certain factors may interfere with the sexual functioning of the aging population. These may include lost opportunities for intimacy because of widowhood or the lack of privacy. Fears and misperceptions about the possibility of enjoying one's sexuality during the latter years stand in the way. Certainly, physical illnesses, surgical procedures, and medications can become obvious barriers to sexual expression. Some of the elderly misinterpret usual and normal physical and bodily changes. Some elderly people fear that intercourse may cause death. Actually, this is quite rare. Depression does increase during the later years of life, which certainly reduces sexual motivation. And the elderly have an increasingly poor self-image as the body shrinks and becomes flabby with loose skin and wrinkles. They are hesitant to allow even their spouse to see parts of their bodies unadorned, let alone revealing themselves in the nude. The elderly may have sexual disorders such as erectile dysfunction, retarded ejaculation, orgasmic dysfunction, or vaginismus. These problems often can be remedied at least in part by using a variety of positions, lubrication, and mutual stimulation. Some fortunate elderly couples discover that a sexual experience can be quite satisfying with only one orgasm or even without either spouse achieving an orgasm. Such couples find that cuddling and touching and caressing and talking can be quite fulfilling and add a great dimension to their intimacy.

Erikson (1963, pp. 268-269) wrote that ego integrity can only occur

> in him who in some way has taken care of things and people and has adapted himself to the triumphs and disappointments adherent to being. . . . It is the acceptance of one's one and only life cycle as something that had to be and that, by necessity, permitted no substitutions. . . . The possessor of integrity is ready to defend the dignity of his own lifestyle against all physical and economic threats . . . in such final consolation, death loses its sting.

Reputation, accomplishments, beauty, influence, affection, wealth—these have been important sources of self-esteem. Christianity proclaims that the real basis of worth lies beyond these things: it is God's love that grounds human dignity and self-worth (Whitehead, 1992, pp. 178, 179).

The Little Boy and the Old Man

Said the little boy, "Sometimes I drop my spoon."
Said the little old man, "I do that too."
The little boy whispered, "I wet my pants."
"I do that too," laughed the little old man.
Said the little boy, "I often cry."
The old man nodded, "So do I."
"But worst of all," said the boy, "it seems
Grown-ups don't pay attention to me."
And he felt the warmth of a wrinkled old hand.
"I know what you mean," said the little old man.

Anonymous

SPIRITUAL INTERESTS

Churches need to keep a great many things in mind to provide a ministry to the aged. Many of the aging have increasing trouble with steps. A ramp or elevator helps, but keeping their programs on the ground floor whenever possible is the best solution. Second, they do not like to go out at night. The lenses of the eye grow yellow or darker each year. By the time one gets past retirement, seeing after dark, even in rather good light, is difficult (Birren and Schaie, 1985, pp. 296-331). This means, of course, that driving after dark becomes increasingly challenging. So, the wise pastor simply schedules all of the activities for the elderly in the daytime. It is difficult for these people to leave the house: to get up, get ready, and find transportation to the church. Once they arrive, they do not mind staying awhile, but after they are dismissed and sent home, it is tough to find the energy to return for an evening service.

Thus, many thoughtful churches provide lunch for this age group, knowing that many of these people do not eat very well anyway. Many live alone or cannot get out to the grocery store. Others have limited money and fixed incomes. A time to be together with friends and others of similar age and interests is important to them. They are hungry for this! They have too little opportunity for it. A number of churches have helped their communities start programs such as meals-on-wheels to see that their elderly members get good food.

Some churches have started a daily phoning system whereby healthy volunteers (often in this age category) telephone from their homes certain numbers of homebound elderly people once or twice each day. This does not take long. If the homebound person can answer the phone, then the volunteer (and the family who has asked for this service) knows that the elderly person is not lying somewhere with a broken bone or unconscious or too sick to answer the phone. If the phone is not answered, the volunteer goes or sends someone to the residence.

DYING: THE FINAL STAGE OF LIFE

I believe (and I have heard many physicians voice the same opinion) that the elderly, especially those who are religious, do not really fear death. On the contrary, many people do fear dying. For many, death comes either too soon or too late. The prolongation of life now possible through advances in medical technology often causes dying to become a protracted, painful, and undignified experience. Fear is widespread among aged people that they will be forced to spend their last days hooked up to complicated medical apparatus, and that their desire to die in a natural and dignified manner will be ignored by hospitals concerned mostly with protecting themselves from litigation. This involves many unknown factors, and the unknown arouses anxiety. The modern hospice movement (Berger, 1988, p. 615) deserves credit for contributing to improvements in these respects throughout our health care system.

One of our early encounters with anxiety at the beginning of life is with separation anxiety. We worry about being separated from our caregivers. We experiment with this in the game that babies in almost all cultures play, called "peek-a-boo." The baby is checking to see if people and things that cannot be seen are actually still there. Psychologists call it "object permanence" (Clarke-Stewart, Perlmutter, and Friedman, 1988, p. 600). We again deal with separation anxiety at the end of life as we prepare to leave family, friends, and this world.

Table 10.2 sets forth the leading causes of death in the United States. Most of us will die of either heart disease or cancer.

TABLE 10.2. Ten Leading Causes of Death in the United States, 1997

Cause of Death	Percentage
Heart Disease	31.4
Cancer	23.2
Stroke	6.9
Chronic Obstructive Lung Diseases	4.8
Accidents	4.0
Pneumonia and Influenza	3.8
Diabetes Mellitus	2.7
Suicide	1.3
Kidney Disease	1.1
Cirrhosis and Chronic Liver Disease	1.1

Source: Adapted from Famighetti (1998), p. 876.

Elisabeth Kübler-Ross (1969), in her book *On Death and Dying,* proposed a stage-based model of dying focused on psychosocial and spiritual dynamics, which has been helpful to many. However, there is no reason to think that humans cope with dying only five ways. Moreover, it is a mistake to expect or, worse, to force all dying persons to go through all five stages and in order. We do need to remember that the dying are still alive and often have unfinished needs which they wish to address. They are grieving, not only the imminent loss of their own lives, but also the loss of their relationships with everyone they know.

Spiritual aspects of coping with dying involve those sources from which one draws spiritual vigor and vitality. The spiritual dimension concerns hope. Hope involves faith and trust and may be directed toward cure/recovery or salvation. It will probably focus in one way or another on relief from distress.

Chapter 11

The Family Life Cycle

Having now moved through the life cycle stage by stage, let us take a brief look at the life cycle of a particular family, considering the processes of system formation and evolution over time. While each family system is going through its life cycle, each individual family member is moving through his or her own personal life cycle. We will study the individuals involved in the context of their family in its developmental process, dealing with the normal issues with which families in general must contend as they grow and evolve.

As Table 11.1 indicates, Stage 1 in the family life cycle is that of the unattached adult. The emotional issues center on the acceptance of parent-offspring separation. The critical tasks include differentiation from family of origin, development of peer relations, initiation of a career, and selection of a spouse.

Thus, we first encounter the relationship system of Rick and Jan, who are both seventeen years old. The two had met during high school at age fifteen. Jan invited Rick to her church, where he experienced a religious conversion. They started dating and were "going steady" at age sixteen. Shortly after turning seventeen, Rick dedicated his life to ministry, thus choosing his career. He began college after finishing his junior year of high school while Jan completed high school. This effectively separated him from his family of origin.

This couple was engaged to be married when Jan's family decided to move to California. The couple fast-forwarded their wedding plans and were married before Jan graduated from high school. Both of their parents had trouble accepting this decision but finally gave their blessing for the wedding. Early marriage was an intergenerational phenomenon in Rick's family.

TABLE 11.1. Stages of the Family Life Cycle

Stage	Emotion Issues	Stage Critical Tasks
1. The Unattached Adult Courtship	Accepting parent-offspring separation.	a. Differentiation from family of origin. b. Development of peer relations. c. Initiation of career.
2. Newly Married Couple Family Formation	Commitment to the marriage.	a. Formation of marital system. b. Making room for spouse with family and friends.
3. Childbearing First Child	Accepting new members into the system.	a. Adjusting marriage to make room. b. Taking on parenting roles. c. Making room for grandparents.
4. Preschool-Age Child Childrearing	Accepting the new personality.	a. Adjusting family systems to needs of a specific child. b. Coping with energy drain and lack of privacy.
5. School-Age Child Multiple Children	Allowing child to establish relationships outside the family.	a. Extending family system to interact with society. b. Encouraging child's educational achievement.
6. Teenage Child First Child Leaves Home	Increasing flexibility of family boundaries to allow child's independence.	a. Shifting parent-child relationship to balance freedom/limits. b. Refocusing on mid-life career and marital issues. c. Beginning concerns for older generation.
7. Launching Center Last Child Leaves Home	Accepting exits from and entries into the family.	a. Releasing young adult children into work, college, and marriage. b. Maintaining a supportive home base.
8. Middle-Age Parents The Empty Nest	Letting go and facing each other again.	a. Rebuilding the marriage. b. Realigning family to include spouses of children and grandchildren. c. Dealing with aging of one's own parents.
9. Retirement and Old Age Contracting Family	Accepting retirement.	a. Adjusting to retirement. b. Coping with death of parents, spouse. c. Closing or adapting family house. d. Maintaining individual and couple functioning. e. Supporting middle generation.

Sources: Adapted from Duvall, 1977; Barnhill and Longo, 1978; Carter and McGoldrick, 1988.

As a newly married couple, Rick and Jan dealt with the Stage 2 emotional issue of commitment to the marriage. Their critical tasks for this phase of the family life cycle included formation of the marital system and making room for the spouse with family and friends. Choosing marriage enabled them to begin the early-adulthood task of embracing intimacy. Each had expectations of the other brought from their respective families of origin. As a married couple, they were experienced differently in their social environment.

Rick accepted the call to become pastor of a small rural church near the college. Rules began to emerge in their relationship that provided time to be both together and apart, either with friends or alone. Jan felt that Rick neglected her too much in order to study. However, in time they worked out mutual support that allowed them to complete routine tasks and still have time to play together. Each found the other interesting to talk to and they enjoyed spending as much time together as possible. They evolved a circle of friends that they were comfortable visiting, and they kept in touch with their families almost every week: all in all, a fairly stable pattern.

After six months of marriage and repeated messages from both sets of parents about the importance of grandchildren, Jan became pregnant. Stage 3 is the childbearing stage, in which the emotional issue is that of accepting new members into the family system. Adjusting the marital relationship to make room for children, taking on parenting roles, and making room for grandparents are the critical tasks. The couple's first son was born just after Rick graduated from junior college. Both were excited about their baby, but they each had some misgivings about their ability to be good parents. Rick experienced some feelings of resentment over the amount of time that Jan devoted to the baby, and he devoted more time to study. Jan was often tired from all her responsibilities of motherhood and was sometimes upset by what appeared to be Rick's lack of interest in their son, who was dealing with the individual issues in the age of grace.

Eventually Jan and Rick were able to work out a new relationship that gave them time to be a couple as well as parents. Almost two years later, they had a second son. Having successfully weathered the crises of parenthood that accompanied the birth of their first baby, they were better able to handle the increasing complexity of their four-member family system. Three years later, Rick had graduated from college, entered seminary, and was pastor of a church when their daughter was born.

As their children grew into toddlers, they encountered Stage 4 of the family life cycle. The family's tasks included adjusting the system to the needs of the individual personalities of each child and coping with the energy drain and lack of privacy as a married couple. Individually, the children were dealing with their first developmental tasks: the age of works and family romance.

When Rick graduated from seminary, the family moved to a distant state for his doctoral studies. During those years a fourth child was born. This family moved into Stage 5 as the children began to start to school. The emotional issue here involves allowing each child to establish relationships outside the family. Stage-critical tasks include engaging the family system with society and encouraging each child's educational achievement. Jan was at first saddened by the children's eagerness to go off each morning, but soon appreciated the extra time, took more courses, and taught children in the seminary laboratory school. Individually, the children were dealing with the developmental tasks in the age of friendships.

Upon completion of his studies, Rick decided to go into chaplaincy and counseling as a career and accepted a job back in their home state. A couple of years later, their fifth child was born.

Jan and Rick entered Stage 6 when their oldest children reached adolescence. With teenage children, the family emotional issue is to increase the flexibility of the family boundaries so the young people can make more decisions for themselves. The stage-critical tasks include shifting the parent-child relationship to balance freedom and limits, refocusing on midlife career and marital issues, and beginning concerns for the older generation. The growing children each continued to work at their respective developmental tasks such as the age of discovery and the age of struggle. The family moved to a small farm within the city limits for a few years during this time. Jan's parents retired, and she completed a professional degree and took a full-time job.

When the two oldest sons started leaving home for college and the military, the family entered Stage 7. The family becomes a launching center and the emotional issue is accepting exits and entries into the family. The tasks involve releasing young adult children into college or work and maintaining a supportive home base. The two oldest sons encountered the developmental tasks in the age of adjustment. Rick and Jan found it hard to believe that so many years had passed and experienced this as a happy-sad time. Routines had to be adjusted. Weddings had to be planned. However, they did find more time to spend having fun with friends and often traveled together to Rick's professional meetings.

After ten years as a hospital chaplain and pastoral counselor, Rick accepted a faculty position and the family moved to an adjoining state. Jan made her own independent decision to move. The two youngest boys were still in grade school. So, this family spent many years in Stages 5 to 7.

Stage 8 is when middle-aged parents must let go of their children and face each other again. Their task is to rebuild their marriage as a two-person system, to realign their family to include the spouses of their children along with grandchildren, and to deal with their own aging parents. Thus, individuals in the family are dealing with the developmental tasks of a number of the life cycle stages during this time. Jan and Rick enjoyed being in-laws and grandparents. Jan's father had a heart attack and died eight years later. Her mother had a stroke and moved into an intermediate care retirement villa. Their youngest child left for college when they were fifty-two years old. Nevertheless, three of their children returned to live at home again before leaving home for good.

Retirement, the final stage in the family life cycle, characterizes Stage 9. Accepting retirement and old age is the emotional issue. Adjusting to retirement, coping with the death of parents (and possibly siblings or spouse), closing or adapting the family house, providing support for the more central role of the middle generation, and maintaining their functioning as individuals and as a couple make up the stage-critical tasks. Jan retired at sixty-two and Rick about a year later. They moved to a lake near where they grew up, which is in the state where four of their five children and seven of their eleven grandchildren live. They spend more time with family than at any time since their children lived at home. Jan seems to have accepted retirement easily and never plans to work again, although she has had problems adjusting to the house they bought. Rick has taken on several part-time jobs much as he used to have and enjoys staying busy. They are active in their church and are making new friends.

The foregoing has been an attempt to illustrate events within the life cycle, both individual and family. Modification of the roles and rules of the relationships of family members are most likely to occur at the points of transition. These changes may cause problems or even crises. Individuals must feel and exhibit much love and determination to keep the family system together.

Chapter 12

History and Theories of Personality Development

A group of people were waiting in line to buy tickets to a movie. Two adolescent boys crowded into the line in front of a middle-aged couple. "I'd like to talk to the parents of those two kids," growled the man to his wife. "And tell them how to raise children," his wife responded, "Boys are like that." Sounding much like Socrates, the man behind them chimed in: "These teenagers are getting worse all the time. They have no manners."

Every one of us has a theory of why people behave as they do. The trouble is that we rarely agree in our explanation of human behavior, and there is no easy way to decide whose idea is correct. Personal theories of development are formulated from private experiences, learning, and beliefs. These are influenced by all kinds of things such as television, movies, reading, and common assumptions in our culture.

Actually our naive "theories" of human growth and personality development are not really theories in the formal, scientific sense. They are often internally inconsistent, and we have not stated them clearly enough to generate testable predictions.

An understanding of the life cycle is important to several disciplines of thought. For religion, questions of "Why am I here?" and "What am I supposed to do with my life?" are important and somewhat different as we move through life. For the humanities, an understanding of the stages of life is central to the question of "Who am I?" Knowledge of growth and development is important to medicine since health, diseases, and treatment vary according to one's age. In ancient Greek mythology, only the tragic hero Oedipus was able to answer the question of the Sphinx: "What walks on four legs in the morning, two legs in the afternoon, and three legs in the evening?"

Our ancestors in the West believed that the conception of the stages of life provided an essential understanding of the interrelationships among people, nature, God, and the cosmos. Hippocrates and Galen, for example, divided human life into stages. Their divisions were adapted and preserved in medieval medicine, natural philosophy, and theology. As early as the twelfth century, sculptors and painters used the stages of life to express symbolic truth about the interrelationships of all creation. In these works, the ages of a person's life correspond to the seasons, the cycle of day and night, animals, or the planets. The motif of the stages of life arose with the invention of the printing press and iconography and could be found in Germany, Italy, the Netherlands, and France during the sixteenth and seventeenth centuries. These artistic renderings always contain a series of figures, each one representing a time of life. The number of stages varied from as few as three to as many as twelve. Often the wheel of fortune was included to imply the theme of circular or cyclical development. Thus, when Eric Erikson described the "Eight Ages of Man" in his book *Childhood and Society* in 1950, he was adding to this historical vision of the life cycle that had captured the conception of life for many centuries.

Psychologists specializing in the area of human growth and development sometimes discuss architectural descriptions of human personality under a heading such as "the structure of personality" (Oates, 1957, pp. 171-196). Theologians approach a similar basic reality under the heading of the Christian doctrine of persons or even Christian anthropology.

The word "personality" is derived from the Latin word *persona*, which means, in its verb form, "to sound through." The word had three usages. It first referred to a mask worn in a drama to represent a character. The word also meant a character or part in a play, and it came to refer to the player who acted the part. Many definitions of personality have been proposed by psychologists. Gordon Allport (1897-1967), a prominent psychologist, discussed over four dozen such definitions (1937). In this book, a simple definition of personality will suffice: an individual's relatively constant way of reacting to the environment.

In this chapter, various models of personality that have influenced theories of development will be presented. We will explore the major types of developmental theories and some of the common assumptions within each type. We will also acknowledge that no theory can explain all human behavior but that each can make a useful contribution.

Figure 12.1 reviews the life line, including the stages of development.

BIBLICAL IDEAS OF WHOLENESS

The Hebrews had no word for personality. Neither did they have a word for body. For them the body was the person and they needed no differentiation between the physical and the mental. A person was thought of as a whole being, a totality. The Hebrew word *nephesh* referred to the inner aspect of the body. It is often translated as "soul," but to read the Greek idea of soul into it is a mistake.

The second basic word in Hebrew psychology was *lev,* usually translated "heart." But in Hebrew thought, the heart was the place where the emotions were located. It also means inner person, mind, or will. The third word was *ruach,* meaning spirit or breath. Thus, a person *(nephesh)* had inner feelings *(lev)* that were exhibited through the spirit *(ruach).*

The New Testament records Jesus as using the Greek word *kardia* in the same sense that the Hebrews used *lev* for heart. Jesus used *psuche* (soul) to mean that which was more precious about life than anything else. He used *pneuma* (spirit or breath) to mean the God-encountering dimension of a person.

In the teachings of Paul, the two Greek words *sarx* (flesh) and less often *soma* (body) were used in a way that corresponds to our word "personality." Paul seemed to avoid coupling the words *soma* and *psuche* for fear of being misunderstood as adhering to the Greek philosophical notion of dualism (to be explained in the next section). He maintained the Hebrew holistic view of persons and preferred to use the words *sarx* and *pneuma* to make that clear.

Another Greek word widely used in the New Testament similar to our use of the word "personality" is *prosopon,* usually translated

FIGURE 12.1. Life Line

Infancy		Childhood		Youth		Adulthood		
Birth 18 mos. 3		6	10	13	20	35	55	70

Prenatal

Grace Works | Family Romance | Friendships | Discovery Struggle Adjustment Achievement Conservation Retirement

Age	Psychosexual Stage	The Age of	Psychosocial Crisis
Birth-18 mos.	Oral-Sensory	Grace	Basic Trust vs. Mistrust
18 mos.-3 years	Anal	Works	Autonomy vs. Shame & Doubt
3-6	Genital	Family Romance	Initiative vs. Guilt
6-10	Latency	Friendships	Industry vs. Inferiority
10-13	Puberty	Discovery	Identity vs. Role Confusion
13-20	Adolescence	Struggle	
20-40	Young Adulthood	Adjustment	Intimacy vs. Isolation
40-60	Middle Adulthood	Achievement	Generativity vs. Stagnation
60-70	Older Adulthood	Conservation	Ego Integrity vs. Despair
70-ff	Maturity	Retirement	

"face" or "countenance." In Matthew 6:16 Jesus spoke of the Pharisees who "disfigure their faces" in fasting to be seen by others, using the word to imply a deceptive mask that hid the real self. In Luke 9:51 Jesus was said to have "set his face" steadfastly to go to Jerusalem, indicating purpose, goal, or intention. In 2 Corinthians 5:12 Paul talked about people boasting on the positions or status they held. And in Galatians 2:11 Paul described his face-to-face encounter with Peter over the latter's having refused to eat with Gentiles. This passage presents selves in relation.

So the Bible maintained a holistic view of the structure of human personality. A person was seen as a unit having thought, emotion, and behavior. Table 12.1 discusses psychosocial, biblical, and theological themes in the life cycle.

PHILOSOPHICAL NOTIONS OF DUALISM

Both naive and scientific observers of human behavior in the past and present all make assumptions, usually unstated, about human development. These sometimes focus on the ease or difficulty of changing behavior (malleability), the active or passive role of a person in his or her own development, the innate goodness or evil in humanity, and the relationship of child to adult behavior.

The Greek philosophers had quite different notions of the structure of personality than did the biblical writers. Plato (422-347 B.C.E.) conceived of the soul as separate and different from the body. He believed that the soul was immortal, existing both before the creation of the body and after its demise. He taught that the soul never dies. Popular Christian thinking seems to largely accept Plato's teaching but mistakenly attributes these ideas to the New Testament.

Aristotle (384-322 B.C.E.) had a more unified understanding of persons and emphasized the inseparability of body and soul. He described the functional aspects of the soul in three ways. For him the nutritive soul was the minimal soul that exists in both plants and animals. The sensitive soul functioned in all animals in such areas of sensory experience as perception, feelings of pleasure or pain, and desiring. The rational soul was the highest nature of persons.

TABLE 12.1. Psychosocial, Biblical, and Theological Themes

Psychosocial Themes[1]	Basic Virtues and Antipathies[1]	Biblical Examples	Biblical Pilgrimage[2]	Beatitudes[2]
Trust vs. Mistrust	Hope vs. Withdrawal	Abraham, Joseph, Jacob, Thomas, Peter, Israelites	Genesis: claiming the world	Pure in heart
Autonomy vs. Shame and Doubt	Will vs. Compulsion	Adam and Eve, Hannah, Samuel, Mary, Moses	Exodus: exploring the world's boundaries	Meek
Initiative vs. Guilt	Purpose vs. Inhibition	David, Peter, Saul/Paul	Leviticus: Learning the world's lawfulness	Hunger and thirst for righteousness
Industry vs. Inferiority	Competence vs. Inertia	Mary and Martha, Jacob, Joseph, Paul, Moses	Numbers: confronting outsiders	Poor in spirit
Identity vs. Identity Confusion	Fidelity vs. Repudiation	Saul/Paul, Jacob/Israel	Deuteronomy: preparing to possess the land	Persecuted for righteousness
Intimacy vs. Isolation	Love vs. Exclusivity	David	Joshua: gaining a foothold	Peacemakers
Generativity vs. Stagnation	Care vs. Rejectivity	Moses, Timothy's mother, invalid by pool	Judges: establishing community	Merciful
Ego Integrity vs. Despair	Wisdom vs. Disdain	Job	Ruth: finding sanctuary	Mournful

[1]Erikson (1982). [2]Capps (1987). [3]Wright (1982). [4]Gleason (1975). [5]Source unknown.

Theological Themes[3]	Theological Themes[4]	Faith Elements[2]	God Representation That Allows Belief[5]	God Representation That Leads to Unbelief[5]
Providence	Doctrine of God	Spirit of expectancy	I am held, fed, nurtured. I see me in your face. You make me in your image.	I am not held. I am hungry. I feel uncared for. I cannot see me (You are not making me).
Grace or Gratefulness	Good and Evil	Spirit of self-mastery	I feel you are with me.	I cannot feel you are there for me. I despair.
Repentance	Sin and Redemption	Spirit of equity	You are wonderful, the Almighty. You are love. You love me.	I thought you were omnipotent. You fail. You do not love me. I do not count.
Vocation	Works	Spirit of self-worth	You are God, my protector.	You are destructive. You won't spare me.
Faith	Doctrine of Man	Spirit of nonconformity	You are the maker of all things. You are the beloved and the loving.	You are unjust. You permit evil. You suffocate me.
Communion	Christology	Spirit of peacemaking	You are. You let me be me.	You think I am a child. Let me be me.
Vocation	Creation	Spirit of empathy	I accept you whatever you are.	You never gave me anything.
Awareness of the Holy	Eschatology	Spirit of longing	Whatever, whoever you are, I trust you.	You are not there.

These views of persons as having a double nature were first set forth by Plato, elaborated by Aristotle, and carried forth through history to the modern age by such eminent thinkers and writers as Thomas Aquinas (1225-1274 C.E.), René Descartes (1596-1650), John Locke (1632-1704), Jean-Jacques Rousseau (1712-1778), and John Dewey (1859-1952). G. Stanley Hall founded the study of developmental psychology in the United States. Throughout, the body was thought of as mostly evil and unchangeable while the soul was pure and undefilable. Some recommended self-discipline or even punishment to correct the body's wrongs. Others suggested allowing the body to satisfy its desires since the soul could not be corrupted anyway. The following proverb suggests methods of approaching man's many dualities:

> There are four sorts of men:
> He who knows not and knows not he knows not:
> He is a fool—shun him;
> He who knows not and knows he knows not:
> He is simple—teach him;
> He who knows and knows not he knows:
> He is asleep—wake him;
> He who knows and knows he knows:
> He is wise—follow him.

Arab Proverb

PSYCHOLOGICAL CONCEPTS OF LEARNING

One of the important assumptions in psychology is that all people have certain basic needs or drives. These must be satisfied in some way for survival and to maintain personhood. Ecclesiasticus (Sirach) 39:26 says, "The basic necessities of human life are water and fire and iron and salt and wheat flour and milk and honey, the blood of the grape and oil and clothing." Thomas Aquinas (*Summa Theologiae,* 1976, I-II, 9.24, a.2) classified the common basic needs as (1) the need to preserve life, (2) the need to procreate, (3) the need to know the truth, and (4) the need to live in society.

One of the questions that is of interest to the fields of religion, moral philosophy, and psychology is how these needs or desires will be fulfilled. A list of basic needs will differ from one theory of personality to another but may include: air, drink and food, rest and sleep, gregariousness and communication, movement and exercise, cleanliness, and sex and love. A well-known formulation of needs is that of Abraham Maslow (1908-1970), in which he conceptualizes needs in pyramid fashion in the following order: survival, safety, social, self-esteem, and self-actualization. Each word represents a category of needs, as shown in Figure 12.2. His assumption is that until the lower needs are satisfied, we cannot concentrate on the higher needs. Maslow's (1970) self-actualization level includes the need to know and understand, to contemplate, and to create. This is the level of commitment, creativity, and transcendence at which persons not only live within a culture, but criticize it, transcend it,

FIGURE 12.2. Maslow's Hierarchy of Needs

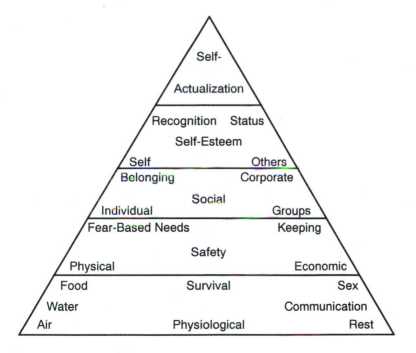

Source: Maslow (1970).

and contribute to it. Human beings have been created with a capacity for spirituality and religion, if they choose to utilize it. However, it is not a basic need that must be fulfilled to be human.

Many learning and behavior theorists such as B. F. Skinner (1904-1990) (Skinner, 1974) or Albert Bandura (1986) think a newborn baby is a relatively empty and passive organism prepared to react to stimulation from its environment. They see development as a continuous process throughout the life span. New behaviors are learned partly because they are rewarded. For instance, children learn to imitate their parents because parents reward attempts to behave in socially acceptable ways. Thus, kids learn to walk, talk, count, read, and write as part of growing up. Adults continue learning because of the rewards that come from acquiring new work or social skills. A presentation of the major concepts of B. F. Skinner and Albert Bandura appears on page 143.

Most learning or behavior theories concentrate on observable behaviors and are not concerned with the inner events of persons that cannot be observed. Some theories, for example, consider mental concepts such as love, maturity, intelligence, and personality as meaningless apart from the behaviors that define them and the situations in which they occur. This approach has provided a useful corrective to the vague, unscientific use of mental concepts that characterized some earlier theories.

Some of these theorists have assumed that all motivation to behave is based on the wish to reduce tension by satisfying the basic needs. Others have expanded their view of maturation to include curiosity and exploration. Thus boredom may lead to a state of arousal that is rewarded by exploration. The attention, praise, and money that a parent or society may give an individual are effective rewards which reinforce behavior.

Behaviorists and learning theorists have distinguished between two kinds of conditioning. Classical or respondent conditioning, first described by Ivan Pavlov (1849-1936) (1902), has been divided into two kinds of reflexes. Unconditional reflexes are natural responses that do not have to be learned, such as salivating at the sight of food. Conditioned reflexes are established when you associate a neutral stimulus such as a noon whistle with an unconditioned stimulus. If the neutral stimulus occurs repeatedly just prior

B. F. Skinner

Major Concepts and Terms

Operant Behavior: behavior determined by its effect on the environment
Functional Analysis: linking a behavior to the precise conditions that determine it
Contingency: the relationship between a behavior and its consequences
Reinforcement: any stimulus that increases the likelihood of a behavior occurring

Emphasis

Concern with overt behavior—what the individual does, how he behaves
Determination of precise environmental conditions or situational events that control or determine behavior
Rejection of inferred dynamics or other internal motivational forces
Application of basic conditioning principles to complex behaviors

Areas of Application

Programmed instruction, self-control, control of institutions, social and environmental engineering

Albert Bandura

Major Concepts and Terms

Observational Learning: learning without any direct rewards or reinforcements
Imitation: learning and performance of a behavior as a consequence of observing another person
Model: a person who provides information about a behavior by performing that behavior
Acquisition Versus Performance: the distinction between learning a behavior and its actual commission

Emphasis

Concern with overt behavior—what the individual does, how he or she behaves
Consideration of internal, cognitive events only in relation to their behavioral referents
Focus on learning in the absence of overt performance and reinforcement
Concern with complex current social behavior, such as skill acquisition

Areas of Application

Acquisition of social behaviors, effects of television, learned aggression and fear, therapeutic intervention

Source: L. Hoffman and S. Paris (1975), in *Developmental Psychology Today,* Second Edition. New York: McGraw-Hill, p. 31. Reprinted with permission of The McGraw-Hill Companies.

to the unconditional stimulus, a person will begin to respond to the neutral stimulus much as he or she originally did to the uncondi- tioned stimulus, i.e., salivation will begin at the sound of the noon whistle.

Emotions are particularly subject to classical conditioning. A child can come to fear the sight of an object that is associated with something that earlier caused him or her pain. A toddler may begin to cry when he or she sees a nurse wearing white because white has previously been paired with painful injections.

Operant or instrumental conditioning changes the frequency of a response as a result of reinforcement or rewards. When a child gets candy or social approval for responding in a certain way, that be- havior will probably be repeated. Responses that are not rewarded or that are punished decrease in frequency or may even be elimi- nated (extinguished). A grade school-age child will learn table man- ners more quickly if praised when performing them and ignored when he or she is not. Imitation also plays a key role in operant conditioning. If a child is rewarded for increasing imitation of cer- tain parental behaviors, the child will show these behaviors even when the parent is not nearby.

Jean Piaget's (1896-1980) view of genetic epistemology presents persons as active seekers of stimulation, and as a filter, organizer, interpreter, and storer of experiences (Piaget, 1970). For him, genetic means developmental and epistemology is the study of knowledge: how we know what we know. A baby acts on nearby objects, feeling, banging, and mouthing them and thereby growing in knowledge by experience. The infant also interacts with people in similar ways. The child grows in the understanding of the world by coordination of actions and the interrelationships of objects. For example, most adults understand gravity. But a year-old baby explores gravity by dropping bits of dinner from the highchair and watching intently as the beans hit the floor. The baby also learns that the food cannot be both dropped and eaten. Equilibration is the most general develop- mental principle in Piaget's theory. It states that an organism always tends toward biological and psychological balance as it progresses but that balance is never fully achieved. A presentation of the major concepts of Jean Piaget appears on page 145.

Jean Piaget

Major Concepts and Terms

Constructionism: the individual's understanding of the world, which arises from patterns of relationships or schemes between objects and actions
Adaptation: the tendency for an organism to maintain equal balance between the processes of assimilation (absorbing and organizing experiences around existing activity patterns) and accommodation (modifying existing activity patterns to allow incorporation of new knowledge)
Stages of Intellectual Development: periods that are not continuous and that are distinctly different over life
Scheme: a pattern of mental action that helps the individual understand the world

Emphasis

Primary concern with understanding how we know what we know; focus on cognitive or mental structure
Belief that knowledge grows from the interaction between the genetically determined cognitive structure of organism and the environment
Emphasis on limitations caused by cognitive structural development
De-emphasis of environmentally produced changes and individual differences

Areas of Application

Education, intelligence, problem solving, communication

Source: L. Hoffman and S. Paris, 1975, p. 31. Reprinted with permission of The McGraw-Hill Companies.

PSYCHOANALYTICAL PRINCIPLES OF DYNAMICS

Psychodynamic theorists have centered their attention on personality development. They analyze development in light of various confrontations between the growing individual, obtaining gratification for the basic needs, and demands of society. Most also emphasize the gradual development of a sense of self, an identity against which to judge one's behavior. They are generally concerned with inner development and especially those early emotional experiences that they assume have influenced later behavior.

Sigmund Freud (1953), the father of psychodynamic theories and the founder of psychoanalysis, has had an enormous influence on the arts and literature as well as psychology. He assumed that from earliest infancy people are motivated by an irrational urge toward pleasure. In Freud's architecture of personality, he proposed three conflicting aspects: the id (it), the superego (above I), and the ego (I). These are inferential concepts. In the id reside all of the unconscious needs and impulses. It is the unknown and unconscious aspect of mental life. The superego is much like the conscience and begins to develop in early childhood as the child internalizes parental values. The ego is most in contact with the world around the person and mediates the repeated internal conflicts between the id and the superego (see Figure 12.3.) Freud described the life cycle in sexual terms, tying psychological development to the resolution of conflicts that characterize each stage of life. The major concepts of Sigmund Freud are presented on page 147.

Harry Stack Sullivan (1953) did not present a neat three-level diagram of the human psyche in his theory. He proposed a structure of personality in terms of a dynamic self-system, which is accrued

FIGURE 12.3. Freud's Architecture of Personality

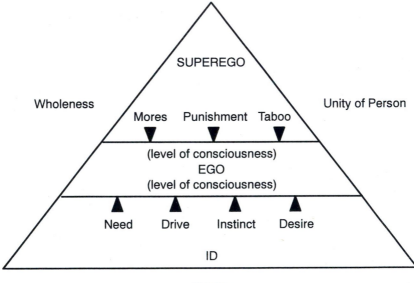

Sigmund Freud

Major Concepts and Terms

Psychic Structure: the organization of the personality, consisting of id, ego, and superego

Anxiety: the experience of discomfort as a consequence of conflict among parts of the psychic structure

Defense Mechanisms: responses that an individual makes in an attempt to cope with and reduce anxiety

Psychosexual Stages: stages of personality development based on different zones of pleasure—oral, anal, phallic, and genital

Emphasis

Concern with intrapsychic dynamics; why people are driven to do what they do

Explanation of behavior through analysis of conflicts among instincts, reality, and society

Belief that instincts and maturational development precede environmental effects

De-emphasis of rational cognitive processes

Areas of Application

Psychotherapy, parent-child relations, abnormal behavior, education

---

Source: L. Hoffman and S. Paris (1975), p. 37. Reprinted with permission of The McGraw-Hill Companies.

through experiences of approval and disapproval in interpersonal relationships. Thus experiences of tenderness and approval are incorporated into an individual's self-system as the "good-me." Disapproval creates anxiety and is experienced as rejection. This is included in the self-system as the "bad-me." Some aspects of the child's or adult's experience such as dreams, fantasies, and mental disorders are incommunicable to self or others. These experiences are called the "not-me." The major concepts of Harry Stack Sullivan are presented on page 148.

Erik Erikson modified Freud's concepts into a psychosocial theory (Roazen, 1997). In it personality develops through eight stages (see Table 12.2), which are predetermined by the person's

---

Harry Stack Sullivan

Major Concepts and Terms

Personification: a group of related attitudes, feelings, and concepts about oneself or another, which have been acquired from extensive experience

Dynamism: an enduring pattern of learned behaviors that recur in an individual's interpersonal relations

Self-structure: defensive behaviors that are learned to avoid or minimize anxiety arising from interpersonal relationships

Experience: events that the individual participates in and that become more distinct and ordered during development

Emphasis

Focus on individual as a product of the interpersonal environment; distinctly human qualities are the consequence of social interaction

Belief that development is sequential, that the individual passes through a series of phases, accumulating experiences from predominant relationships

Belief that tension and anxiety arise from the individual's interaction with the environment

Equal emphasis on rational cognitive processes and on irrational emotional processes

Areas of Application

Psychotherapy, interpersonal communication, parent-child relations, education

---

Source: L. Hoffman and S. Paris (1975), p. 37. Reprinted with permission of The McGraw-Hill Companies.

readiness to interact with a widening social world. Development consists of the progressive resolution of conflicts between the child's needs and social demands. Failure to resolve problems at any stage can result in psychological disorders that will affect the rest of life. The major concepts of Erik Erikson are presented on page 150.

The family life cycle is the newest paradigm in human growth and development. The fact that families change over time has been obvious. However, systematic study of family changes has increased the ability of family systems theorists to understand, pre-

TABLE 12.2. Erikson's Eight Stages of Personality Development

Stage	Crisis	Virtue
maturity	ego integrity vs. despair	wisdom
adulthood	generativity vs. stagnation	care
young adulthood	intimacy vs. isolation	love
puberty and adolescence	identity vs. identity diffusion	fidelity
latency	industry vs. inferiority	com-petence
locomotive-genital	initiative vs. guilt	purpose
muscular-anal	autonomy vs. shame, doubt	will
sensory-anal	basic trust vs. mistrust	hope

Source: Adapted from Erikson (1979), p. 61.

Erik Erikson

Major Concepts and Terms

Psychosocial Development: human development viewed in terms of its
    dependence on interaction with others
Crisis: the critical conflict that an individual experiences as he or she
    grows emotionally
Stages of Growth: crucial periods in development, each consisting of
    unique conflicts that an individual must deal with
Ego Identity: the accumulated, integrated experiences of the individual's
    view of the self

Emphasis

Concern with psychosocial development throughout life and with the role
    of society and interpersonal relationships in individual development
Belief that growth occurs out of the confrontation between an individual's
    needs and the demands of society
Belief that an individual's social view of himself or herself is more impor-
    tant than his sexual urges
Emphasis on continuity between the stages of development

Areas of Application

Psychotherapy, parent-child relations, psychiatry, education

Source: L. Hoffman and S. Paris (1975), p. 37. Reprinted with permission of
The McGraw-Hill Companies.

dict, and influence those changes. The cornerstones upon which
Bowen's (1978) family systems theory is based are the concepts of
(1) differentiation of the self, (2) anxiety due to emotional fusion,
(3) triangulation, (4) family projection process, (5) emotional cut-
off, and (6) multigenerational transmission. The family life cycle
acknowledges that various members of a family are in different
stages of development at any given time. Yet, they all interact and
influence one another. Families must successfully (more or less)
accomplish their developmental tasks to secure individual satisfaction, gain social approval, and move on to the next stage.

SUMMARY

Although the theories presented in this chapter may appear to have nothing in common, they are largely complementary. Theory can be seen as eclectic and integrative. All agree that human growth is regular and that behavior is potentially predictable.

All theories of human development are based on different assumptions about the nature of persons. Behavior-learning theories view people's behavior as quite malleable, their role in development as passive, and the development of behavior as continuous over the life span. Piaget, on the other hand, thought human behavior was relatively changeable, their role in development was active, and that development occurred in stages. Psychodynamic theories see the behavior of persons as relatively fixed, with the development of how one feels about oneself as of great importance while the individual follows a developmental course toward becoming an active, complete person. Family systems theorists emphasize the social interactions of family members as they move through the developmental stages.

So, what is developmental psychology? One book has summarized it succinctly as follows (Clarke-Stewart, Perlmutter, and Friedman, 1988, pp. 23, 24):

Development implies that the change is systematic, not random; that it is permanent, not temporary; that it is progressive, not regressive—it goes forward not backward; that it is steady, not fluctuating; that it occurs in regular, predictable order; that it occurs over some period of time within a person's lifetime, not in an hour or over two generations; that it occurs for all people, not just a few; and perhaps most centrally, that it is related to a person's increasing age and experience.

The domain of development contains several areas:

1. Physical development, including bodily changes and motor development
2. Emotional development, including expression of feelings and correct labeling
3. Cognitive development, including thought and language

4. Social development, including interactions and relations with others
5. Religious development, including belief, faith, and practice

We have considered all of these in this book. We have noticed individual differences again and again. The further we develop and grow, the more we become uniquely like ourselves—the person God created us to become, and the better we get at loving and working.

LANDMARKS OF LIFE

The rarity of miracles
       is doubted by few.
Save those who stare deeply
       into eyes that are blue.
Tears fall as he squints
       at the bright light in fear.
And wonders and shivers
       as a voice meets his ear:
"My son, my miracle, my love, you are here."

* * *

His skin soft as cotton
       but wrinkled and wet
As innocent and quiet
       as a child could get
He stares through those slits
       and scrambles for thoughts
And forms his first memories
       his belly in knots
He screams in confusion: "What has destiny brought?"

* * *

Through his fear of unknowns,
       spies he one striking face.

In her arms he feels warmth
        and his heart 'gins to race.
Held tight to her breast
        he feels her heart pound
His eyes become heavy,
        mind spinning around.
When they shut, he dreams only
        of colors and sounds.

* * *

As time races onward,
        how quickly he grows
He studies his discovery
        of fingers and toes.
Rolling over, he coos
        and gurgles and plays
And pees and poops
        and screams where he lays.
He knows they will come—he's studied their ways.

* * *

When he discovers his balance,
        he sits, then he stands.
Clumsy but curious
        are his sweet little hands.
He conquers the stairs
        then his bladder and stool
And learns by mistakes,
        as he conquers preschool
Since attachment to mother is no longer the rule.

* * *

Independent at eight,
        he frolics through June
With lemonade stands
        and Saturday cartoons.

The cuts and the bruises
        of each arm and leg
Mark an adventure, a victory,
        a battle, a plague.
And, when called in at dusk, it's more time that he begs.

* * *

Though the adventures continue,
        time does not wait.
Though Mom wishes him smaller,
        growth is his fate.
Sprouting above her
        much more is he taught.
Defending beliefs
        hard battles are fought.
So much to consider, while lost in his thoughts.

* * *

Face riddled with pimples
        he clashes and fights.
They just do not fathom
        the extent of his plight.
His life seems as Hell
        and his questions abound
Asking: "Why is there Life?"
        and: "Where am I bound?"
But, in the midst of despair, true Love has he found.

* * *

Well, the seasons they change
        and the years they pass
The boy becomes man
        and graduates his class.
And, for the woman beside him,
        the Love of his Life

He proclaims his Love
        and makes her his wife.
And they face Life together, the challenge and strife.

* * *

They work for good credit
        and to buy a nice home
An auto with airbags,
        a vacation in Rome.
And, as his parents before him,
        he wishes and prays
He trusts in the miracles
        of God's loving ways.
And a blessing arrives on a wintry day.

* * *

She stares with blue eyes
        and studies his face
Then drifts into sleep
        in his loving embrace.
The three become four
        and then become five
How lucky he is
        to be blessed with their lives.
For their safety and happiness is all that he strives.

* * *

Through good times and bad,
        through stitches and flu
He absorbs all their fears
        as a father should do.
And as they grow older
        and each takes their leave
He beams with pride
        at the success they achieve
And only the death of his youth does he grieve.

* * *

Time spares no man
      and holds back the years
The last child leaves
      as he fights back the tears.
But strong he remains
      as each wrinkle peaks
And to look twenty-seven
      is all that he seeks.
"It's your time to be old," reminds his bones with a 'creak.'

* * *

As sure as life starts,
      it surely must end.
He bows his head thoughtfully,
      bids farewell to a friend.
His parents are gone now
      he misses them so
The children are grown
      his longing they know
And, the grandkids—amazing, how quickly they grow.

* * *

The days become longer
      and he feels trapped beneath
No more comes the tooth fairy
      to trade for his teeth.
His cabinet is weighted
      with bottles and vials
Blood pressure and sugar
      reflect daily trials.
And his bowels have not moved for a very long while.

* * *

With a tear in his eye
        he sends off his Love
And prays for a rendezvous
        somewhere above.
In loneliness he dwells
        with each passing day
His hearing and eyesight
        have faded away.
And, had he the company, he'd have nothing to say.

* * *

His innocence now lost,
        his memories now fade,
His destiny now sure,
        and he surely afraid.
His joints are all painful,
        his head how it pounds
Neither sees he, nor hears he
        his family around.
And he bids them farewell, without uttering a sound.

* * *

Tears fall as he squints
        at the bright light in fear
And wonders and shivers
        as a voice meets his ear:
"My son, my miracle, my love, you are here."

P. Douglas Kelley
April, 1991
SIU-SM

Bibliography

Aden, L., Benner, D.G., and Ellens, J.H. (Eds.). (1992). *Christian Perspectives on Human Development*. Grand Rapids, MI: Baker.

Allport, G. (1937). *Personality: A Psychological Interpretation*. New York: Holt.

Allport, G. (1955). *Becoming: Basic Considerations for a Psychology of Personality*. New Haven, CT: Yale University Press.

Allport, G. (1961). *Pattern and Growth in Personality*. New York: Holt, Rinehart, and Winston.

Ambron, S.R. and Brodzinsky, D. (1979). *Lifespan Human Development*. New York: Holt, Rinehart and Winston.

Andry, A.C. and Schepp, S. (1968). *How Babies Are Made*. New York: Time-Life.

Aquinas, T. (1976). *Summa Theologiae*. Gilby, T. (Ed.). New York: McGraw-Hill.

Aristotle. (1950). *Politics*. McKeon, R. (Ed.). Chicago: University of Chicago.

Associated Press (1991). Survey: Americans waiting to say "I Do." Springfield, IL: *State Journal-Register,* June 7, p. 4.

Augustine. (1961). *The Confessions of Saint Augustine*. Pusey, E.B. (Trans.). New York: Collier.

Axinn, W. and Thornton, A. (1992). The Relationship Between Cohabitation and Divorce. *Demography, 229*(3): 357-374.

Aylward, G.P. (1991). Behavioral and developmental disorders of the infant and young child: Assessment and management. In D.E. Gerydydanus and M.L. Wolraich (Eds.), *Behavioral Pediatrics*. New York: Springer-Verlag.

Azrin, N.H. and Foxx, R.M. (1974). *Toilet Training in Less Than a Day*. New York: Simon and Schuster.

Bach, G. and Wyden, P. (1969). *The Intimate Enemy: How to Fight Fair in Love and Marriage*. New York: Morrow.

Baldwin, W. and Nord, C. (1984). Delayed childbearing in the U.S.: Facts and fictions, *Population Bulletin, 39*(4): 42.

Ballard, R.E. (1983). *Clergy and the Mental Health of Families*. Columbus, GA: Brentwood.

Baltes, P.B. and Brim, O.G. Jr. (1982). *Life-Span Development and Behavior*. New York: Academic.

Bandura, A. (1986). *Social Foundation of Thought and Action*. Englewood Cliffs, NJ: Prentice-Hall.

Bardill, D. (1997). *The Relational Systems Model for Family Therapy*. Binghamton, NY: The Haworth Press, Inc.

Barnhill, L.R. and Longo, D. (1978). Fixation and Regression in the Family Life Cycle. *Family Process, 17*(4): 469-478.

Berger, K.S. (1988). *The Developing Person Through the Life Span,* Second Edition. New York: Worth.

Bergler, E. (1954). *The Revolt of the Middle-Aged Man.* New York: Wyn.

Berndt, T.J. and Ladd, G. (1988). *Peer Relationships in Child Development.* Somerset, NJ: Wiley.

Berne, E. (1967). *Games People Play.* Boston: Allyn and Bacon.

Bianchi, E.C. (1984). *Aging As a Spiritual Journey.* New York: Crossroad.

Billingham, K.A. (1982). *Developmental Psychology for the Health Care Professions: Part I: Prenatal Through Adolescent Development.* Boulder, CO: Westview.

Birren, J. and Schaie, K. (Eds.) (1985). *Handbook of the Psychology of Aging.* New York: Van Nostrand Reinhold.

Block, J. and Haan, N. (1971). *Lives Through Time.* Berkley, CA: Bancroft.

Botwinick, J. (1973). *Aging and Behavior.* New York: Springer.

Bowen, M. (1978). *Family Therapy in Clinical Practice.* New York: Jason Aronson.

Breuer, J. and Freud, S. (1936). *Studies on Hysteria,* A. Brill (Trans.). New York: Nervous and Mental Disease Pub. Co.

Bridges, W. (1980). *Transitions: Making Sense of Life's Changes.* Reading, MA: Addison-Wesley.

Bright Futures, National Maternal and Child Health Clearinghouse, 2070 Chain Bridge Road, Suite 450, Vienna, VA 22182, <www.brightfutures.org>.

Bromley, D.B. (1966). *The Psychology of Human Aging.* Baltimore: Penguin.

Browning, D.S. (1973). *Generative Man: Psychoanalytic Perspectives.* Philadelphia: Westminster.

Brunner, B. (Ed.) (1997). *1998 Information Please Almanac.* Boston: Information Please LLC.

Brunner, B. (Ed.) (1998). *The Time Almanac 1999.* Boston: Information Please LLC.

Calkins, E., Davis, P.J., and Ford, A.B. (1986). *The Practice of Geriatrics.* Philadelphia: Saunders.

Capps, D. (1983). *Life Cycle Theory and Pastoral Care.* Philadelphia: Fortress Press.

Capps, D. (1987). *Deadly Sins and Saving Virtues.* Philadelphia: Fortress Press.

Carlsen, M.B. (1988). *Meaning-Making: Therapeutic Processes in Adult Development.* New York: Norton.

Carter, E.A. and McGoldrick, M. (Eds.) (1988). *The Changing Family Life Cycle: A Framework for Family Therapy,* Second Edition. New York: Gardner.

Case, R. (1985). *Intellectual Development: Birth to Adulthood.* New York: Academic.

Chapko, J.J. (1985). *Faith in Search of a Focus: An Internal Critique of the Faith Development Theory of James Fowler.* Toronto: Institute for Christian Studies.

Chew, P. (1976). *The Inner World of the Middle-Aged Man.* New York: Macmillan.

Clarke-Stewart, A., Perlmutter, M., and Friedman, S. (1988). *Lifelong Human Development.* New York: Wiley.

Claypool, J. (1977). *Stages.* Waco, TX: Word.

Clinebell, H. and Clinebell, C. (1970). *The Intimate Marriage.* New York: Harper & Row.

Cobble, J.F. (1985). *Faith and Crisis in the Stages of Life.* Peabody, MA: Hendrickson.

Colarusso, C.A. (1992). *Child and Adult Development: A Psychoanalytic Introduction for Clinicians.* New York: Plenum.

Coleman, L.E. Jr. (1982). *Understanding Today's Adults.* Nashville, TN: Convention.

Commons, M.L., Sinnott, J.D., Richards, F.A., and Armon, C. (1989). *Adult Development: Comparisons and Applications of Developmental Models.* New York: Praeger.

Cook, J.K. and Moorehead, L.C. (1990). *Six Stages of a Pastor's Life.* Nashville, TN: Abingdon.

Cox, R.D. (1970). *Youth into Maturity: A Study of Men and Women in the First Ten Years After College.* New York: Mental Health Materials Center.

Crystal, J.C. and Bolles, R.N. (1974). *Where Do I Go from Here with My Life?* New York: Seabury.

Cumming, E. and Henry, W. (Eds.) (1961). *Growing Old: The Process of Disengagement.* New York: Basic Books.

Dacey, J.S. (1982). *Adult Development.* Glenview, IL: Scott, Foresman.

Daniels, P. and Wengarten, K. (1983). *The Timing of Parenthood in Adult Lives.* New York: Norton.

Davitz, J. and Davitz, L. (1976). *Making It from Forty to Fifty.* New York: Random.

Dayringer, R. (1996). Homosexuality reconsidered. *Journal of Pastoral Care, 50*(1): 57-71, Spring.

Dayringer, R. (1998). *The Heart of Pastoral Counseling,* Revised Edition. Binghamton, NY: The Haworth Press.

de Castillejo, I.C. (1973). *Knowing Women.* New York: Harper & Row.

Demetrious, A., Dois, W., Van Lieshout, A., and Cornelis, F. (1998). *Lifespan Developmental Psychology: Normative Life Crises.* New York: Wiley.

Droege, T.A. (1966). A Developmental View of Faith. Unpublished doctoral dissertation. Chicago: Divinity School, University of Chicago.

Droege, T.A. (1974). A developmental view of faith. *Journal of Religion and Health.* 3:313-29.

Duvall, E. (1977). *Marriage and Family Development,* Fifth Edition. Philadelphia: Lippincott.

Dykstra, C.R. (1981). *Vision and Character: A Christian Educator's Alternative to Kohlberg.* New York: Paulist.

Dykstra, C.R. and Parks, S. (Eds.) (1986). *Faith Development and Fowler.* Birmingham, AL: Religious Education.

Egan, G. and Cowan, M.A. (1980). *Moving into Adulthood.* Monterey, CA: Brooks/Cole.

Elder, G.H. Jr. (Ed.) (1985). *Life Course Dynamics.* Ithaca, NY: Cornell University Press.

Elkin, D. and Hetzel, D. (1977). *Readings in Human Development*. New York: HarperCollins.

Elkind, D. (1974). *Children and Adolescents: Interpretive Essays on Jean Piaget, Second Edition*. New York: Oxford University Press.

Envoy, J.J. and Christoph, V.F. (1963). *Personality Development in the Religious Life*. New York: Sheed and Ward.

Erikson, E.H. (1963). *Childhood and Society*, Revised Edition. New York: Norton.

Erikson, E.H. (1967). *Identity: Youth in Crisis*. New York: Norton.

Erikson, E.H. (1979). Reflections on Dr. Borg's Life Cycle. In D. Van Tassel (Ed.), *Aging, Death and the Completion of Being*. Philadelphia: University of Pennsylvania.

Erikson, E.H. (1980). *Identity and the Life Cycle*. New York: Norton.

Erikson, E.H. and Erikson, J. (1974). *Vital Involvement in Old Age*. New York: Brunner/Mazel.

Erikson, E.H. and Erikson, J.M. (1982). *The Life Cycle Completed: A Review*. New York: Norton.

Famighetti, R. (Ed.) (1998). *The World Almanac and Book of Facts 1999*. Mahwah, NJ: World Almanac Books.

Feldman, H.S. and Lopez, M.A. (1982). *Developmental Psychology for the Health Care Professions*. Boulder, CO: Westview.

Field, T.M., Huston, H.Q., Troll, L., and Finly, G. (Eds.) (1982). *Review of Human Development*. New York: Wiley.

Flexner, A. (1910). *Medical Education in the United States and Canada: A Report to the Carnegie Foundation for the Advancement of Teaching*. Bulletin No. 4. Boston: Updyke.

Formanek, R. (1990). *The Meanings of Menopause: Historical, Medical and Clinical Perspectives*. Hillsdale, NJ: Analytic.

Fowler, J.W. (1981). *Stages of Faith: The Psychology of Human Development and the Quest for Meaning*. San Francisco: Harper & Row.

Fowler, J.W. (1984). *Becoming Adult, Becoming Christian: Adult Development and Christian Faith*. San Francisco: Harper & Row.

Fowler, J.W. (1987). *Faith Development and Pastoral Care*. Philadelphia: Fortress.

Fowler, J.W., Keen, S., and Berryman, J. (1980). *Life Maps: Conversations of the Journey of Faith*. Waco, TX: Word.

Fraiberg, S.H. (1959). *The Magic Years: Understanding and Handling the Problems of Early Childhood*. New York: Scribners.

Franzblau, R.N. (1971). *The Middle Generation*. New York: Holt.

Freud, S. (1933). *New Introductory Lectures on Psychoanalysis*, Sprott, W. (Trans.). New York: Norton.

Freud, S. (1938). *The Basic Writings of Sigmund Freud*, A. Brill (Ed.). New York: Modern Library.

Freud, S. (1953). *A General Introduction to Psychoanalysis*, Riviere, J. (Trans.). New York: Permabooks.

Fried, B.R. (1967). *The Middle-Aged Crisis*. New York: Harper & Row.

Fuchs, E. (1977). *The Second Season.* Garden City, NY: Anchor/Doubleday.

Fuller, R.C. (1988). *Religion and the Life Cycle.* Philadelphia: Fortress.

Gaylin, W. (1990). *Adam and Eve and Pinocchio: On Being and Becoming Human.* New York: Viking.

Gemelli, R. (1996). *Normal Child and Adolescent Development.* Washington, DC: American Psychiatric Press.

Gerzon, M. (1996). *Listening to Midlife.* Boston: Shambhala.

Giele, J.Z. (Ed.). (1982). *Women in the Middle Years.* New York: Wiley.

Gilligan, C. (1982). *In a Different Voice: Psychological Theory and Women's Development.* Cambridge, MA: Harvard University Press.

Gleason, J. (1975). *Growing Up to God.* Nashville, TN: Abingdon.

Golan, N. (1983). *Passing Through Transitions.* Riverside, NJ: Free Press.

Goldman, R. (1964). *Religious Thinking from Childhood to Adolescence.* New York: Seabury.

Goldman, R. (1965). *Readiness for Religion: A Basis for Developmental Religious Education.* New York: Seabury.

Gordon, T. (1975). *P.E.T.: Parent Effectiveness Training.* New York: New American Library.

Gould, R. (1978). *Transformations: Growth and Change in Adult Life.* New York: Simon and Schuster.

Greeley, A. (1995). *Sex: The Catholic Experience.* New York: Thomas More.

Greenspan, S.I. and Pollock, G.H. (Eds.) (1980). *The Course of Life: Psychoanalytic Contributions Toward Understanding Personality Development, III: Adulthood and the Aging Process.* Adelphi, MD: NIMH.

Groeschel, B.J. (1983). *Spiritual Passages: The Psychology of Spiritual Development.* New York: Crossroad.

Group for the Advancement of Psychiatry. (1989). *Psychiatric Prevention and the Family Life Cycle.* New York: Brunner/Mazel.

Gubrium, J.F. and Buckholdt, D.R. (1977). *Toward Maturity.* Washington, DC: Jossey-Bass.

Hall, G. (1922). *Senescence: The Last Half of Life.* New York: Appleton-Century-Crofts.

Hallborg, E.C. (1977). *The Grey Itch: The Male Menopause Syndrome.* Granite Bay, CA: Ombudsman.

Hamilton, L.S. (1955). *Your Rewarding Years.* New York: Bobbs-Merrill.

Havighurst, R.J. (1972). *Developmental Tasks and Education,* Third Edition. New York: McKay.

Havighurst, R.J. and Albrecht, R. (1953). *Older People.* New York: Longmans.

Heidi, G. (1976). *Winning the Age Game.* Garden City, NY: Doubleday.

Hennig, M. (1970). Career Development for Women Executives. Doctoral dissertation. Cambridge, MA: Harvard University.

Hennig, M. and Jardin, A. (1977). *The Managerial Woman.* New York: Doubleday.

Herbert, J.I. (1989). *Black Male Entrepreneurs and Adult Development.* New York: Praeger.

Hightower, J.E. Jr. (1985). *Caring for Folks from Birth to Death.* Nashville, TN: Broadman.

Hinders, N. (1994). *Seasons of a Woman's Life: Autumn, Winter, Spring, Summer: Life is a Recurring Series of Transitions.* Nashville: Broadman and Holman.

Hippocrates (1988). *The Writings of Hippocrates on the Human Body,* Adams, F. (Trans.). Albuquerque, NM: American Classical College Press.

Hoffman, L. and Paris, S. (1975). *Developmental Psychology Today,* Second Edition. New York: McGraw-Hill.

Holy Bible, New Revised Standard Version (1989). New York: National Council of Churches.

Horowitz, F.D. (1987). *Exploring Developmental Theories: Toward a Structural/ Behavioral Model of Development.* Hillsdale, NJ: Erlbaum.

Howe, R.L. (1967). *The Creative Years.* New York: Seabury.

Howells, J.G. (Ed.) (1981). *Modern Perspectives in the Psychiatry of Middle Age.* Philadelphia: Brunner/Mazel.

Hudson, R.L. (1955). *Growing a Christian Personality.* Nashville, TN: Sunday School Board.

Hunt, B. and Hunt, M. (1975). *Prime Time: A Guide to the Pleasures and Opportunities of the New Middle Age.* New York: Stein and Day.

Ivey, A.E. (1986). *Developmental Therapy: Theory into Practice.* New York: Jossey-Bass.

Jakobovits, T. (1970). The treatment of impotence with methyltestosterone thyroid. *Fertility and Sterility, 21*(1): 32-35.

James, M. (1979). *Marriage Is for Loving.* Reading, MA: Addison-Wesley.

Jaques, E. (1973). Death and the mid-life crisis. In Ruitenbeck, H.M. (Ed.), *The Interpretation of Death*, pp. 140-165. New York: Aronson.

Johnson, S. (1989). *Christian Spiritual Formation in the Church and Classroom.* Nashville, TN: Abingdon.

Joy, D.M. (Ed.) (1983). *Moral Development Foundations: Judeo-Christian Alternatives to Piaget/Kohlberg.* Nashville, TN: Abingdon.

Jung, C.G. (1957). *The Undiscovered Self*, R. Hull (Trans.). New York: American Library.

Jung, C.G. (1969). The Stages of Life. In *Collected Works of C.G. Jung*, Volume 8. R.F.C. Hull (Trans.). Princeton, NJ: Princeton University Press.

Jung, C.G. (1971). Marriage as a psychological relationship. In Campbell, J. (Ed.), *The Portable Jung.* New York: Viking.

Kail, R.V. and Cavanaugh, J.C. (1996). *Human Development.* New York: Brooks/ Cole.

Kaluger, G. and Kaluger, M. (1974). *The Span of Life.* St. Louis: C.U. Mosby.

Kao, C.C. (1975). *Search for Maturity.* Philadelphia: Westminster.

Kao, C.C. (1981). *Psychological and Religious Development: Maturity and Maturation.* Washington, DC: University Press.

Kegan, R. (1982). *The Evolving Self: Problem and Process in Human Development.* Cambridge, MA: Harvard University Press.

Kimmel, D.C. (1990). *Adulthood and Aging: An Interdisciplinary Developmental View.* New York: Wiley.

Kinsey, A., Pomeroy, W., and Martin, C. (1948). *Sexual Behavior in the Human Male.* Philadelphia: Saunders.

Kinsey, A., Pomeroy, W., Martin, C., and Gebhard, P. (1953). *Sexual Behavior in the Human Female.* Philadelphia: Saunders.

Koenig, H. (1994). *Aging and God.* Binghamton, NY: The Haworth Press.

Koenig, H., Lamar, T., and Lamar, B. (1997). *A Gospel for the Mature Years.* Binghamton, NY: The Haworth Press.

Kohlberg, L. (1963). Development of children's orientation toward a moral order. *Vita Humana,* 6:11-36.

Kohlberg, L. (1973). Continuities in childhood and adult moral development revisited. in P. Baltes and K. Schaie (Eds.), *Lifespan Developmental Psychology: Personality and Socialization,* p. 202ff. New York: Academic.

Kohlberg, L. (1974). Education, moral development, and faith. *Journal of Moral Education,* 4(1):5-16.

Kohlberg, L. (1976). Moral stages and moralization. In T. Likona (Ed.), *Moral Development and Behavior: Theory, Research, and Social Issues.* New York: Holt, Rinehart, and Winston.

Kohlberg, L. (1981, 1984). *Essays on Moral Development,* Vols. 1 and 2. New York: Harper & Row.

Konner, M. (1991). *Childhood.* Boston: Little, Brown.

Kübler-Ross, E. (1969). *On Death and Dying.* New York: Macmillan.

Kuhn, D. (1984). Cognitive development. In M.H. Bornstein and M.E. Lamb (Eds.), *Developmental Psychology: An Advanced Textbook.* Hillsdale, NJ: Erlbaum.

Kurtines, W.M. and Gewirtz, J.L. (1984). *Morality, Moral Behavior, and Moral Development.* New York: Wiley.

Landis, J.T. and Landis, M.G. (1963). *Building a Successful Marriage,* Fourth Edition. Englewood Cliffs, NJ: Prentice-Hall.

Laumann, E., Michael, K., Michael, S., and Gagnon, J. (1994). *The Social Organization of Sexuality.* Chicago: University of Chicago.

Lawrence, D.H. (1982). *Sons and Lovers.* New York: Penguin.

Lazarus, L.W. (1988). *Essentials of Geriatric Psychiatry.* New York: Springer.

LeBoyer, F. (1975). *Birth Without Violence.* New York: Knopf.

Lerner, R.M. (1986). *Concepts and Theories of Human Development,* Second Edition. New York: Random House.

LeShan, E.J. (1973). *The Wonderful Crisis of Middle Age.* New York: McKay.

Levine, M.D., Carey, W.B., and Crocker, A.C. (1992). *Developmental Behavioral Pediatrics,* Second Edition. Philadelphia: Saunders.

Levinson, D.J., Darrow, C.N., Klein, E.B., Levinson, M.H., and McKee, B. (1978). *The Seasons of a Man's Life.* New York: Knopf.

Levinson, D.J. and Levinson, J.D. (1996). *The Seasons of a Woman's Life.* New York: Ballantine.

Lewis, M. and Vokmar, F. (1990). *Clinical Aspects of Child and Adolescent Development,* Third Edition. Philadelphia: Lea & Febiger.

Lidz, T. (1968). *The Person.* New York: Basic.

Locke, J. (1690/1998). Essay concerning human understanding. New York: Viking Penguin.

Losoncy, L. (1977). *Religious Education and the Life Cycle.* Bethlehem, PA: Catechetical Communications.

Lowenthal, M.F., Fiske, M.T., and Chiriboga, D. (1976). *Four Stages of Life.* San Francisco: Jossey-Bass.

Lyon, K.B. (1985). *Toward a Practical Theology of Aging.* Philadelphia: Fortress.

Madden, M.C. and Madden, M.B. (1980). *For Grandparents: Wonders and Worries.* Philadelphia: Westminster.

Mahler, M.S., Pine, F., and Bergman, A. (1975). *The Psychological Birth of the Human Infant.* New York: International Universities.

Maier, H.W. (1965). *Three Theories of Child Development.* New York: Harper & Row.

Manaster, G.J. (1977). *Adolescent Development and the Life Tasks.* Boston: Allyn and Bacon.

Maslow, A. (1968). *Toward a Psychology of Being,* Second Edition. New York: Van Nostrand.

Maslow, A. (1970). *Motivation and Personality,* Second Edition. New York: Harper and Row.

Masters, W.H. and Johnson, U.E. (1966). *Human Sexual Response.* Boston: Little, Brown.

Masters, W.H., Johnson, V.E., and Kolodny, R.C. (1986). *Masters and Johnson on Sex and Human Loving.* Boston: Little, Brown.

Matthews, S.H. (1986). *Friendships Through the Life Course.* Beverly Hills, CA: Sage.

McBride, A.B. (1973). *The Growth and Development of Mothers.* New York: Harper and Row.

McCoy, V.R., Ryan, C., and Lichtenberg, J.W. (1978). *The Adult Life Cycle: Training Manual and Reader.* Lawrence, KS: University of Kansas.

McCrae, R. and Costa, P. Jr. (1984). *Emerging Lives, Enduring Disposition: Personality in Adulthood.* Boston: Little, Brown.

McCullough, C. (1983). *Heads of Heaven; Feet of Clay.* New York: Pilgrim.

McKinney, J.P., Fitzgerald, H.E., and Strommen, E.A. (1977). *Developmental Psychology: The Adolescent and Young Adult.* Homewood, IL: Dorsey.

McLeish, J.A.B. (1976). *The Ulyssean Adult—Creativity in the Middle and Later Years.* New York: McGraw-Hill Ryerson.

McMorrow, F. (1974). *Midolescence: The Dangerous Years.* New York: Quadrangle/New York Times.

Moran, G. (1983). *Religious Education Development: Images for the Future.* Minneapolis, MN: Winston.

Muncie, J., Wetherell, J., Dallos, R., and Cochrane, A. (Eds.) (1995). *Understanding the Family.* London: Sage.

Murphy, G. (1949). *Historical Introduction to Modern Psychology,* Revised Edition. New York: Harcourt, Brace & Co.

Murphy, S.M. (1983). *Midlife Wanderer: The Woman Religious in Midlife Transition.* Whitinsville, MA: Affirmation.

Nash, R. (1990). Life's major spiritual issues. *The Caregiver Journal.* 7(1): 3-20.

National Council on Aging. (1975). *The Myth and Reality of Aging in America.* Washington, DC: NCOA.

Nelson, C.E. (1989). *How Faith Matures.* Louisville: Westminster/Knox.

Neugarten, B.L. (1968). *Middle Age and Aging: A Reader in Social Psychology.* Chicago: University of Chicago.

Newman, B.M. and Newman, P.R. (Eds.) (1976). *Development Through Life: A Case Study Approach.* Homewood, IL: Dorsey.

Newman, B.M. and Newman, P.R. (1995). *Development Through Life: A Psychosocial Approach,* Sixth Edition. Pacific Grove, CA: Brooks Cole.

Nouwen, H. (1976). *Aging: The Fulfillment of Life.* Garden City, NY: Image.

Oates, W.E. (1957). *The Religious Dimensions of Personality.* New York: Association Press.

Offer, D. and Sabshin, M. (Eds.) (1984). *Normality and the Life Cycle.* New York: Basic Books.

O'Neill, N. and O'Neill, G. (1974). *Shifting Gears.* New York: Avon.

Oring, E. (1997). *The Jokes of Sigmund Freud.* New York: Jason Aronson

Pavlov, I. (1902). *The Work of the Digestive Glands,* W.H. Thompson (Trans.). London: Griffin.

Peters, D.L. and Willis, S.L. (1978). *Early Childhood.* Monterey, CA: Brooks/Cole.

Peterson, R. (1967). *New Life Begins at Forty.* New York: Trident.

Phares, V. (1995). *Fathers and Developmental Psychopathology.* New York: Wiley.

Piaget, J. (1970). *The Science of Education and the Psychology of the Child,* D. Coltman (Trans.). New York: Orion.

Piaget, J. (1977). *The Development of Thought: Equilibration of Cognitive Structures,* A. Rosin (Trans.). New York: Viking.

Pinson, W.M. Jr. (1981). *The Biblical View of the Family.* Nashville, TN: Convention.

Poland, R.G. (1974). *Human Experience: A Psychology of Growth.* St. Louis: Mosby.

Pulaski, M.A.S. (1980). *Understanding Piaget: An Introduction to Children's Cognitive Development,* Revised Edition. New York: Harper and Row.

Rakel, R. (Ed.) (1995). *Textbook of Family Practice,* Fifth Edition. Philadelphia: W.B. Saunders.

Rank, O. (1994). *The Trauma of Birth.* Mineola, NY: Dover.

Religious Education Association (1987). *Faith Development in the Adult Life Cycle.* Minneapolis: Religious Education Association.

Roazen, P. (1997). *Erik H. Erikson: The Power and Limits of a Vision.* New York: Aronson.

Rogers, D. (1979). *The Adult Years.* Englewood Cliffs, NJ: Prentice-Hall.

Rosenberg, E.B. (1992). *The Adoption Life Cycle: The Children and Their Families Through the Years.* New York: Free Press.

Rossi, A.S. (Ed.) (1985). *Gender and the Life Course.* New York: de Gruyter.

Ruebsaat, H.J. and Hull, R. (1975). *The Male Climacteric.* New York: Hawthorne.

Salholz, E. (1986). Too late for Prince Charming. *Newsweek,* June 2, pp. 54-61.

Santrock, J.W. (1992). *Life-Span Development,* Fourth Edition. Dubuque, IA: Brown.

Scarf, M. (1980). *Unfinished Business: Pressure Points in the Lives of Women.* New York: Doubleday.

Schachtel, E.G. (1954). *Metamorphosis: On the Development of Affect, Perception, Attention, and Memory.* New York: Basic.

Schrier, R.W. (Ed.) (1990). *Geriatric Medicine.* Philadelphia: Saunders.

Selman, R.L. (1980). *The Growth of Interpersonal Understanding.* New York: Academic.

Shakespeare, W. (1917). *The Complete Works of William Shakespeare.* New York: Black.

Sheehy, G. (1974). *Passages: Predictable Crises of Adult Life.* New York: Bantam.

Sheehy, G. (1995). *New Passages.* New York: Ballantine.

Sheehy, G. (1998). *Understanding Men's Passages.* New York: Random House.

Sheffield, M. (1972). *Where Do Babies Come From?* New York: Knopf.

Sherrill, L.J. (1951). *The Struggle of the Soul.* New York: Macmillan.

Simon, A.W. (1968). *The New Years: A New Middle Age.* New York: Knopf.

Skinner, B.F. (1974). *About Behaviorism.* New York: Knopf.

Smith, R.K. (1975). *49 and Holding.* New York: Two Continents.

Smolak, L. (1993). *Adult Development.* Englewood Cliffs, NJ: Prentice-Hall.

Soddy, K. and Kidson, M.C. (1967). *Men in Middle Life.* Philadelphia: Lippincott.

Still, H. (1977). *Surviving the Male Mid-Life Crisis.* New York: Crowell.

Stokes, K. (1989). *Faith Is a Verb: Dynamics of Adult Faith Development.* Mystic, CO: Twenty-Third Publications.

Stoudemire, A. (Ed.) (1998). *Human Behavior: An Introduction for Medical Students,* Third Edition. Philadelphia: Lippincott-Raven.

Stott, L.H. (1974). *The Psychology of Human Development.* Chicago: Holt, Rinehart, and Winston.

Strom, R.D., Bernard, H.W., and Strom, S.K. (1987). *Human Development and Learning.* New York: Human Services Press.

Strommen, M.P. (1971). *Research on Religious Development: A Comprehensive Handbook.* New York: Hawthorne.

Strunk, O. Jr. (1965). *Mature Religion: A Psychological Study.* New York: Abingdon.

Sugar, M. (Ed.) (1993). *Female Adolescent Development,* Second Edition. New York: Brunner/Mazel.

Sullivan, H.S. (1953). *The Interpersonal Theory of Psychiatry,* H.S. Perry and M.L. Gawel (Eds.). New York: Norton.

Swift, J. (1726/1997). *Gulliver's Travels.* New York: Macmillan.

Sze, W.C. (Ed.) (1975). *Human Life Cycle.* New York: Aronson.

Taylor, J. (1982). *The Rule and Exercises of Holy Living.* Ridgefield, CT: Morehouse.

Thomas, A. and Chess, S. (1986). *Temperament in Clinical Practice.* New York: Guilford.

Tizard, L.J. and Guntrip, H.J.S. (1960). *Middle Age.* Great Neck, NY: Channel.

Toman, W. (1993). *Family Constellation.* Fourth Revised Edition. New York: Springer.

Tournier, P. (1972). *Learn to Grow Old*, Hudson, E. (Trans.). New York: Harper and Row.

Troll, L.E. (1973). *The Best Is Yet to Be—Maybe.* Monterey, CA: Brooks/Cole.

Vaillant, G.E. (1977). *Adaptation to Life.* Boston: Little, Brown.

Viorst, J. (1973). *How Did I Get to Be 40 and Other Atrocities.* New York: Simon and Schuster.

Viorst, J. (1986). *Necessary Losses.* New York: Ballantine.

Walsh, F. (Ed.) (1982). *Normal Family Processes.* New York: Basic.

Wesley, F. and Sullivan, E. (1986). *Human Growth and Development: A Psychological Approach*, Second Edition. New York: Human Sciences Press.

Westerhoff, J. (1976). *Will Our Children Have Faith?* New York: Seabury.

Whitehead, E.E. (1992). *Christian Life Patterns.* New York: Crossroad.

Whitehead, E.E. and Whitehead, J.D. (1979). *Christian Life Patterns.* Garden City, NY: Doubleday.

Whitehead, E.E. and Whitehead, J.D. (1984). *Seasons of Strength: New Visions of Adult Christian Maturing.* Garden City, NY: Doubleday/Image.

Winnicott, D.W. (1965). *The Maturational Processes and the Facilitating Environment.* New York: International Universities.

Worthington, E.L. Jr. (1989). Religious faith across the life span: Implications for counseling and research. *The Counseling Psychologist, 17*(4): 555-612.

Wright, J. (1982). *Erikson: Identity and Religion.* New York: Seabury.

Zeahnah, C.H. (Ed.) (1993). *Handbook of Infant Mental Health.* New York: Guilford.

Index

Page numbers followed by the letter "f" indicate figures; those followed by the letter "t" indicate tables.

Wesley, F., 27
Westerhoff, J. E., 61
Whitehead, E. E., 2, 14, 121, 123
Winnicott, D. W., 30
Wisdom, 108, 118, 119
Withdrawal, 69
Women
  crossroads for, 23-24
  lifestyles of, 10-11
  special, 9
  transient, 4

Work, 13, 23, 66, 99, 101, 114, 115, 152
Works, age of, 37-49, 130
Worship, 110-111
Wright, J., 138

Zone, erogenous
  anal, 41, 52
  genital, 52
  oral, 25, 28, 52

THE HAWORTH PASTORAL PRESS
Pastoral Care, Ministry, and Spirituality
Richard Dayringer, ThD
Senior Editor

LOSSES IN LATER LIFE: A NEW WAY OF WALKING WITH GOD, SECOND EDITION by R. Scott Sullender. "Continues to be a timely and helpful book. There is an empathetic tone throughout, even though the book is a bold challenge to grieve for the sake of growth and maturity and faithfulness.... An important book." *Herbert Anderson, PhD, Professor of Pastoral Theology, Catholic Theological Union, Chicago, Illinois*

CARING FOR PEOPLE FROM BIRTH TO DEATH edited by James E. Hightower Jr. "An expertly detailed account of the hopes and hazards folks experience at each stage of their lives. Your empathy will be deepened and your care of people will be highly informed." *Wayne E. Oates, PhD, Professor of Psychiatry Emeritus, School of Medicine, University of Louisville, Kentucky*

HIDDEN ADDICTIONS: A PASTORAL RESPONSE TO THE ABUSE OF LEGAL DRUGS by Bridget Clare McKeever. "This text is a must-read for physicians, pastors, nurses, and counselors. It should be required reading in every seminary and Clinical Pastoral Education program." *Martin C. Helldorfer, DMin, Vice President, Mission, Leadership Development and Corporate Culture, Catholic Health Initiatives—Eastern Region, Pennsylvania*

THE EIGHT MASKS OF MEN: A PRACTICAL GUIDE IN SPIRITUAL GROWTH FOR MEN OF THE CHRISTIAN FAITH by Frederick G. Grosse. "Thoroughly grounded in traditional Christian spirituality and thoughtfully aware of the needs of men in our culture.... Close attention could make men's groups once again a vital spiritual force in the church." *Eric O. Springsted, PhD, Chaplain and Professor of Philosophy and Religion, Illinois College, Jacksonville, Illinois*

THE HEART OF PASTORAL COUNSELING: HEALING THROUGH RELATIONSHIP, REVISED EDITION by Richard Dayringer. "Richard Dayringer's revised edition of *The Heart of Pastoral Counseling* is a book for every person's pastor and a pastor's every person." *Glen W. Davidson, Professor, New Mexico Highlands University, Las Vegas, New Mexico*

WHEN LIFE MEETS DEATH: STORIES OF DEATH AND DYING, TRUTH AND COURAGE by Thomas W. Shane. "A kaleidoscope of compassionate, artfully tendered pastoral encounters that evoke in the reader a full range of emotions." *The Rev. Dr. James M. Harper, III, Corporate Director of Clinical Pastoral Education, Health Midwest; Director of Pastoral Care, Baptist Medical Center and Research Medical Center, Kansas City Missouri*

A MEMOIR OF A PASTORAL COUNSELING PRACTICE by Robert L. Menz. "Challenges the reader's belief system. A humorous and abstract book that begs to be read again, and even again." *Richard Dayringer, ThD, Professor and Director, Program in Psychosocial Care, Department of Medical Humanities; Professor and Chief, Division of Behavioral Science, Department of Family and Community Medicine, Southern Illinois University School of Medicine*

Order Your Own Copy of
This Important Book for Your Personal Library!

LIFE CYCLE
Psychological and Theological Perceptions

_____ in hardbound at $49.95 (ISBN: 0-7890-0171-3)

_____ in softbound at $22.95 (ISBN: 0-7890-0905-6)

COST OF BOOKS_____

OUTSIDE USA/CANADA/
MEXICO: ADD 20%_____

POSTAGE & HANDLING_____
*(US: $3.00 for first book & $1.25
for each additional book)
Outside US: $4.75 for first book
& $1.75 for each additional book)*

SUBTOTAL_____

IN CANADA: ADD 7% GST_____

STATE TAX_____
*(NY, OH & MN residents, please
add appropriate local sales tax)*

FINAL TOTAL_____
*(If paying in Canadian funds,
convert using the current
exchange rate. UNESCO
coupons welcome.)*

☐ **BILL ME LATER:** (\$5 service charge will be added)
(Bill-me option is good on US/Canada/Mexico orders only;
not good to jobbers, wholesalers, or subscription agencies.)

☐ Check here if billing address is different from
shipping address and attach purchase order and
billing address information.

Signature_____

☐ **PAYMENT ENCLOSED: $**_____

☐ **PLEASE CHARGE TO MY CREDIT CARD.**

☐ Visa ☐ MasterCard ☐ AmEx ☐ Discover
☐ Diner's Club

Account # _____

Exp. Date _____

Signature _____

Prices in US dollars and subject to change without notice.

NAME _____

INSTITUTION _____

ADDRESS _____

CITY _____

STATE/ZIP _____

COUNTRY _____ COUNTY (NY residents only) _____

TEL _____ FAX _____

E-MAIL_____
May we use your e-mail address for confirmations and other types of information? ☐ Yes ☐ No

Order From Your Local Bookstore or Directly From
The Haworth Press, Inc.
10 Alice Street, Binghamton, New York 13904-1580 • USA
TELEPHONE: 1-800-HAWORTH (1-800-429-6784) / Outside US/Canada: (607) 722-5857
FAX: 1-800-895-0582 / Outside US/Canada: (607) 772-6362
E-mail: getinfo@haworthpressinc.com
PLEASE PHOTOCOPY THIS FORM FOR YOUR PERSONAL USE.

BOF96